Praise for *Graduate a CEO* and Jim Hunter

"More often than not, college students don't take advantage of their time at university in exploring their entrepreneurial passions. *Graduate a CEO* provides a great step-by-step approach to launching a new business with an early emphasis on feasibility and customer discovery. Any student that's interested in launching a business should use this guide to explore their entrepreneurial passions."

James N. Zebrowski Jr.
Executive Director, Collegiate Entrepreneurs' Organization, Inc.
Tampa, Florida

"Jim Hunter is the consummate entrepreneur and teacher. His clear, easy-to-apply advice will inspire young adults to become all they can be."

Alan Katz
Founder, Katz Bagels, Inc.
President, Katz Consulting
Milwaukee, Wisconsin

"In his book, *Graduate a CEO: Why College Is the Perfect Time to Start Your Business*, Jim Hunter gives a clear and inspiring road map for college students to become successful entrepreneurs. The book is based on the author's distilled practical wisdom gained from his own successful serial entrepreneurship experience and from years of teaching excellence in entrepreneurship courses, insights from judging numerous student new-venture business plan competitions, and guiding scores of entrepreneur interns at a major university. For Jim Hunter, nurturing students' entrepreneurial spirit and helping them to launch well-planned, high-potential start-ups are an important mission, and his book reaches out to fulfill it very effectively!"

V. Kanti Prasad
Past Dean, Lubar School of Business
University of Wisconsin–Milwaukee

"I enthusiastically endorse Jim's book, *Graduate a CEO*. For many of our students, the best part of their education is learning precisely these out-of-the-classroom applications of the concepts and tools they are learning in their courses. Jim has packaged the essential how-tos of becoming an entrepreneur while in college in a highly readable, useful book that all students should read."

Mark Mone
Chancellor, University of Wisconsin–Milwaukee

"Having worked with countless young people interested in starting their own businesses through various programs and academic courses, a proper curriculum or readings have been lacking. With *Graduate a CEO*, Jim Hunter offers budding entrepreneurs an essential and heartfelt guide to the business start-up as a college student. Students may see themselves in these pages and be inspired to take their ideas and passions to the next step. Thanks for writing this important book."

Scott Niederjohn
Professor of Economics and Director, Free Enterprise Center
Concordia University Wisconsin
Mequon, Wisconsin

Moving forward in turbulent and changing times is difficult. *Graduate a CEO* is a refreshingly easy guide on how to do it well. This is a must-read for any student entrepreneur.

Kauchal Chari
Dean, Lubar School of Business
University of Wisconsin–Milwaukee

Jim Hunter and I go back over thirty years when he first asked me to guest lecture his entrepreneur class. His passion and great skill for enlightening students on the art of achieving business success places him in the league of outstanding educators. With *Graduate a CEO,* Jim again is on the money, as he offers leaders an essential and heartfelt guide to a business start-up as a college student. Enjoy the read!

Paul Stewart
Owner, PS Capital Partners
Milwaukee, Wisconsin

Graduate a CEO by Jim Hunter is a hands-on practical book on the entrepreneurial journey. Whether starting a business while in college or simply having the mindset of growth that every entrepreneur should have, this book is must-read. It can be argued that one is never fully ready to be an entrepreneur, as the journey most of the time is on roads less traveled. Remember, every challenge is an unforeseen opportunity, and there's no better way to learn about this journey than through the lens of a proven entrepreneur and teacher of entrepreneurship such as Jim.

Jerry Jendusa
Cofounder, Stuck Breakthrough Strategies
Author and serial entrepreneur
Milwaukee, Wisconsin

Graduate a CEO contains a lifetime of Jim Hunter's relevant personal experiences, keen insights, and practical advice that will assist aspiring entrepreneurs to conceptualize their business, guide them in developing a strategic business plan, and show them how to rapidly test its validity in the market. Jim can help you get to your business destination faster, cheaper, and smarter.

David Lubar
President and CEO, Lubar & Company

GRADUATE A CEO

WHY COLLEGE *is the* PERFECT TIME *to* START YOUR BUSINESS

JAMES H HUNTER III

Advantage.

Published by Advantage, Charleston, South Carolina.
Member of Advantage Media Group.

ADVANTAGE is a registered trademark, and the Advantage colophon is a trademark of Advantage Media Group, Inc.

Printed in the United States of America.

10 9 8 7 6 5 4 3 2 1

ISBN: 978-1-64225-212-5
LCCN: 2022910627

Cover design by Matthew Morse.
Layout design by Wesley Strickland.

This publication is designed to provide accurate and authoritative information in regard to the subject matter covered. It is sold with the understanding that the publisher is not engaged in rendering legal, accounting, or other professional services. If legal advice or other expert assistance is required, the services of a competent professional person should be sought.

Advantage Media Group is a publisher of business, self-improvement, and professional development books and online learning. We help entrepreneurs, business leaders, and professionals share their Stories, Passion, and Knowledge to help others Learn & Grow. Do you have a manuscript or book idea that you would like us to consider for publishing? Please visit **advantagefamily.com**.

To my wife, Betty, my soul mate and confidante for over sixty years. And to my daughter, Sue, and my two sons, Jim and Tom, who have also contributed, earning money to support the family during tough times and giving moral support and advice when I really needed it.

CONTENTS

ACKNOWLEDGMENTS

I am indebted to the students at the University of Wisconsin–Milwaukee and at universities throughout the country who have offered their entrepreneurship stories for this book. They have experienced what it takes to be a student entrepreneur and have been willing to tell their stories. These stories give confidence to new students who may not have considered the prospect of starting their own business while in college. Such a start could bring lifelong satisfaction. Often the business started in college is not the one that the student entrepreneur moves into as the student matures as an entrepreneur. Stories told in this book of many successful entrepreneurs describe several early ventures that just served as learning experiences until a "breakout" venture is started and substantial success is achieved. The learning that takes place within the shelter of the university can provide the foundation for future entrepreneurial success.

Chancellor Mark Mone has been a strong advocate of entrepreneurship at the University of Wisconsin–Milwaukee. He has entertained students engaged in the Student Startup Challenge (a program that supports students who are interested in starting a business while in college) and engages community leaders to support UWM's entrepreneurial thrust. His enthusiasm for entrepreneurship has helped obtain resources to support entrepreneurship such as the Lubar Entrepreneurship Center and academic support, adding faculty focused on entrepreneurship.

Dean Kachal Chari, as the leader of the Lubar School of Business, has supported entrepreneurship by adding faculty dedicated to teaching entrepreneurship and by creating an incubator for development of student businesses at UWM.

Retired Lubar School of Business Dean V. Kanti Prasad has been a strong advocate of entrepreneurship education at the UWM. He has taught entrepreneurship courses and has initiated several competitive activities wherein students gained experience and obtained funding for their ventures.

James N. Zebrowski Jr., the executive director of Collegiate Entrepreneurs' Organization, Inc., in Tampa, Florida, has been extremely helpful in facilitating my making connections with outstanding student entrepreneurs who have been a part of the Global CEO reach. We are very grateful to James for his support in making these network connections.

There are many professionals who have contributed: Darcy Johnson, CFO of Tomach, Inc., and also a key member of the staff of Dynatrap®, provided much material for the ethics chapter. My partners and coowners of Dynatrap, Juan Rocha (the best sales and marketing executive I've ever met) and Dean Johnson (who skillfully ran the operations of Dynatrap)—two great executives who joined with me to build a really great company. Alan Katz and Bruce Paler, entrepreneurs and consultants who provided wisdom and experience as entrepreneurs and mentors. John Schliesmann, senior attorney and wonderful personal advisor to me as we started, developed, and sold Dynatrap. Melissa Zabkowicz, attorney with Reinhart Boerner Van Deuren s.c., provided important legal input. Brian Thompson, who has written the foreword, has contributed to the entrepreneurial ecosystem at the University of Wisconsin–Milwaukee and much of the entrepreneurship thrust in the Milwaukee area. Many other professionals and entrepreneurs added valuable input.

The writing, editorial, and publishing staff of Advantage Media Group, Inc., especially Tanya Martin, Beth Cooper, Laura Grinstead, and Laura Rashley, contributed substantially to the writing and development of the manuscript.

FOREWORD

My career has brought me to a fortunate intersection of discovery, innovation, and entrepreneurship. As director of the Lubar Entrepreneurship Center at the University of Wisconsin–Milwaukee (UWM) and president of the UWM Research Foundation, I have the pleasure of working with hundreds of inventors and entrepreneurs and helping them create and grow new enterprises.

We have a goal of transforming our institution and making entrepreneurship part of every student's journey. This goal is grounded in the belief that our graduates will be more successful if they are able to identify opportunities, develop scalable and sustainable models, and implement change—regardless of their chosen discipline.

Change does not come easily at a large institution, even with visionary supporters and leaders. I recall an idea from my own time in business school that in order to achieve change, one should "stay with the outs." I've always interpreted this to mean one must find and embrace the change agents. I was fortunate to meet Jim Hunter early in my journey at UWM more than fifteen years ago. As someone who knows the value of entrepreneurship, he has been central to our small but growing group of change agents. Together, we are creating and embedding entrepreneurship programs that span departments and colleges and reach students at different levels.

The Lubar Entrepreneurship Center would not be possible without the vision of Sheldon B. Lubar, and he likes to quote his father in noting "a dollar that you earn working for yourself is better than two dollars earned working for someone else." I think the statement goes well beyond the financial implications (think ordinary income versus capital gains). The lessons, benefits, and rewards of entrepreneurship are far reaching.

In this book, Jim highlights how you can start a business in college and why it makes sense. At UWM, we are using entrepreneurship as a learning tool, and not every student will go on to launch a business. For those who do, they will experience the excitement, fear, joy, and transformation that goes along with launching a business. If you want to experience that journey, this book is for you.

When I talk with students and researchers about entrepreneurship and approaches such as lean launch, I like to quip that "it ain't rocket science." I started my career as a systems engineer building and launching communications satellites, so it is with some credibility that I make that assessment. It turns out that even rocket science isn't "rocket science." It is a process of breaking down complex problems into a series of smaller solvable problems. That is what Jim has done with this book—taken a whole range of issues around becoming an entrepreneur and launching a business and broken it down into a series of small and understandable elements.

In this book, you'll also find powerful examples of students who launched businesses while still in college. Examples are powerful, but sometimes they fall victim to a selection bias where only the successful ones are celebrated. But here you'll find stories of genuine individuals who have experienced success and failure as part of their own entrepreneurial journeys.

There is no more powerful example of entrepreneurship than that of Jim Hunter. He has persevered through failure and found success. He has also dedicated himself to inspiring and teaching others. Jim has touched many students in his more than two decades of teaching, and those who return to tell their story are quick to acknowledge the impact Jim had on their entrepreneurial journey.

It's not just in the classroom. Jim has worked with student organizations to achieve scale beyond just those who take his classes, and he has been recognized nationally for his work with those organizations in helping inspire a generation of entrepreneurs.

As you set out on your own entrepreneurial journey, you will find this book to be a valuable resource. And you will find it to be an inspiration as you strive to achieve the rewards that can only come by creating and growing your own business. Good luck on your journey.

Brian Thompson
Director, Lubar Entrepreneurship Center
President, UWM Research Foundation

INTRODUCTION

You may be new to college and sitting in your dorm room or apartment wondering how you can have fun while making your money go further. Or maybe you're a junior or senior thinking about employment prospects after graduation. What if the skills you've obtained in college are not in much demand or the employment prospects don't excite you? Have you considered starting your own business?

Many college students working toward a degree in a particular discipline have little knowledge of the prospects for financial success in their chosen field. The thought of starting a business has not crossed their minds. However, college students with motivation and drive are missing a valuable opportunity if they do not consider starting a business while still in school.

But I'm Not an Entrepreneur!

You may have been one as a kid and just not thought of yourself that way. Maybe you and a friend had a lemonade stand. Maybe you mowed lawns or shoveled snow for neighbors. Maybe you made and

1

sold craft items at a local fair. Whatever you did, you recognized a need and filled it by offering a product or service that had value. If you planned and executed well, you reaped a profit. If you didn't, you (or your parents) lost money. It was your first lesson in free enterprise. Now might be an ideal time to remember this lesson.

> *For an activity to be truly entrepreneurial, it must both fill a valid need and generate a profit.*

In some cases, the entrepreneurship bug continues as the years go by and young people continue to look for opportunities to offer useful products or services that can be profitable. For an activity to be truly entrepreneurial, it must both fill a valid need and generate a profit. The profit earned is the capital that allows the venture to endure and grow. If the venture is well managed, the owner may reap significant financial rewards. But not all entrepreneurs become wealthy. Some incur substantial losses and never recover. Others incur substantial losses, and over time they recover and continue their entrepreneurial activities. A few become successful entrepreneurs from day one, but these instances are rare. It usually takes a failure or two (or more) to galvanize the person to learn from past mistakes and become successful in a new venture.

Student Entrepreneurship

Each semester, I give an interactive lecture on entrepreneurship for freshmen in the Lubar School of Business at the University of Wisconsin–Milwaukee. Upon questioning these students, I find that starting a business while in college is usually not something they've even thought about. This is understandable, since students face many new experiences as they start their college careers. However, because colleges and universities provide abundant opportunities for education and funding relative to new business start-ups, creating a venture while in college should be on a new student's radar. Campus contacts and programs provide access to information, expertise, finances, and other resources; formal and informal learning opportunities; and potential mentors and partners. I've written this book to highlight many of these opportunities that often go unexplored.

My Story

I became an entrepreneur while growing up on a farm in northern Ohio. We had apple, peach, and cherry trees, all producing fruit that we sold at a hand-built fruit stand by the road in front of our house. There was not much investment on my part. The trees bore more fruit than our family could consume, and all that was required was my time to help pick the fruit and work the stand, selling to customers who stopped by. I earned a small amount of cash, and the fruit stand didn't expand into a growing business. But I did gain experience in setting prices, ensuring supply, providing customer service, and handling cash—all valuable lessons for a budding entrepreneur. In high school, I worked for a delicatessen and a greenhouse and earned significantly greater income at these jobs.

My entrepreneurial interest remained dormant for several years after my high school graduation. I attended college and obtained a bachelor of science degree in civil engineering from Purdue University, spending my summers taking jobs with major corporations or on US Navy cruises. After graduation, I was then commissioned as an officer in the Civil Engineer Corps of the US Navy, serving three years of shore-station active duty, and attended graduate school at Harvard Business School to obtain an MBA.

After the US Navy and after obtaining my MBA, I worked at an electronics manufacturing company and then at an industrial products company. I also spent three years in management consulting. Then the entrepreneurial spirit emerged again. The urge to have my own business was so strong that I jumped at the first opportunity that presented itself. A failing company had been run by the trust department of a bank for several years. The company was losing money, sales were dropping, and the organization was in disarray. The company was located in Chicago, and I lived in Milwaukee, ninety miles away. I commuted and struggled with the company for three years. It finally failed, and I lost everything except my house and car.

Here is an event that was important to me as I went through the business failure. On Thursday, December 16, 1976, I received a call from Mike Gutowski of Vince's Sales and Service in Baltimore, Maryland. He told me that my business's customer service was terrible, the product quality was poor, and our prices were not so good. He went on to say that I should get on my knees and pray for guidance. This conversation was a shock to me, but I closed my office door and did as he had asked. I can say that the difficulties we incurred as the business failed did not abate, but I received a feeling of calm and support for myself and my family as we went through this business failure. A few years later I saw Mike at an industry trade conference and thanked him for his phone call. He did not remember the call. I guess he must have made many calls to those needing his advice at that time, and I was fortunate to have been one of those.

After the business failure, my wife started a wallpapering business, my teenage daughter started a house-cleaning business, my older son started a driveway-sealing business, and my four-year-old son started doing his own laundry. I started a new business selling the same products my company had previously manufactured but bought from competitors and private branded. I also began working for a management consulting firm and teaching at the University of Wisconsin–Milwaukee (UWM). These activities allowed me to continue my entrepreneurial pursuits while earning enough income to keep the family afloat.

In subsequent years, I started several more businesses. The most recent business I started and sold was a mosquito-trap business that I established with partners. We obtained a unique mosquito trap made in China and sold it to major retailers throughout North America. The business was started in 2010 and sold in 2019 for over $40 million. It was an excellent product, and the team we assembled to run the business was outstanding.

I continue to teach an entrepreneurship course at UWM, and the experiences I've had during my teaching years have provided material for many cases that I produced for use in the class (Financial Forecasting Case, Bank Loan Committee Case, Bankruptcy Case, Business Valuation Case, Business Purchase Negotiation Case, Franchising Case, Intellectual Property Cases, Legal Forms of Organization Cases, Sales Negotiation Case, and others). To date, more than two thousand students have completed this course, and many have started their own businesses.

Student Stories

Among the thousands of students who have taken my course and others I've come to know, there are some outstanding examples of entrepreneurship. Many of these successful business owners have provided input for this book. Others featured in this book are individuals who excelled at student entrepreneurship and presented winning elevator pitches at the Global Collegiate Entrepreneurs' Organization Conference held each fall and earned other student entrepreneur awards.

Every year, students present elevator pitches at universities throughout the country. The Global Collegiate Entrepreneurs' Organization Conference held by the organization of that name based in Tampa, Florida, holds a conference every year that showcases over one hundred entrepreneur elevator pitches from colleges and universities all over the US to narrow the field down to a handful who compete for a $10,000 prize. This competition is enthusiastically attended by hundreds of students drawn to this conference each year. Successful businesses often are created as a result of the elevator pitches.

Just a few notable examples of these student competition winners are the following:

- **Josh Doering** grew up in a farm community and noticed that farmers were getting injured because they were trying to move a heavy seed slide by climbing up and reaching out to move a lever. It was an awkward maneuver on an elevated ladder, and it was a formula for creating an injury. Josh developed a remote-controlled operator for the lever so that the farmer could operate the bin from a remote location (usually just a few feet away from the bin while standing on the ground). He successfully produced and marketed the product, sold over fifty units, and then sold the company. It was a win for the student and for the customers, who obtained a safe and efficient means of directing seeds into the bin. Josh's venture was also a winner in an elevator pitch competition.

- **Brendan** developed a product that helped him cure an addiction to vaping. The solution offered by Brendan to vaping addiction is called CAPNOS Zero. This device simulates the experience of vaping with harmless but satisfying results. The company's prototypes have been shown to reduce vaping usage from one pod a day down to one a week! Brendan recognizes that much of vaping is a behavioral habit, and he is committed to bringing each customer the right solution to help them quit. He says that the Zero makes quitting fun and easy. In addition to having a winning elevator pitch, Brendan launched his business, and you can visit his website (https://mycapnos.com/) to see his product.

- **Brodie Kerst**, an architecture student at UWM, won the student entrepreneur of the year award by presenting his drone-produced architectural videos for marketing purposes. He became skilled at drone-produced videos, and while he was a student, he sold his services to architectural firms.

It is my own entrepreneurial drive combined with so many inspiring entrepreneurial students that compels me to write this book. I am grateful to all the students for their enthusiasm and willingness to share their stories—stories that I hope will inspire you to begin thinking like an entrepreneur.

CHAPTER 1

WHAT ARE THE CHALLENGES AND REWARDS OF ENTREPRENEURSHIP?

My entrepreneurial spirit really came alive after graduating with my MBA and spending a few years in electronics manufacturing, materials management, and finally top-level organization design and staffing and materials management systems consulting. In fact, the urge to have my own business was so strong that I jumped at the first opportunity that presented itself without taking the time or engaging the appropriate professionals to determine if this was a solid business venture. It wasn't, and when it failed, I lost everything except my house and my car. The impact on my family was substantial. My wife started a wallpapering business, my daughter started a house-cleaning business, and my son started a driveway-sealing business. I became engaged in three activities: managing a new business selling the same products of the previous company, working on management consulting assignments, and participating as adjunct faculty at the local university. It was stressful for the entire family, but we all pitched in to maintain a minimal family income level, and over time, things improved.

I want to help potential entrepreneurs like you avoid my devastating (and avoidable) failure. That you have picked up *Graduate a CEO* and begun to read it is a good sign that you are already ahead of the game. Now, let's get started.

What does it mean to become an entrepreneur? *Entrepreneur* is defined as a person who establishes and manages a new profit-making business, usually bearing all or most of the risks and benefiting from the rewards. Before we go much further, let me note that I believe there is no such thing as a nonprofit entrepreneur. While nonprofit organizations involve utilizing many skills of an entrepreneur, the difference is the profit-making motivation and discipline. It is often said that you must "do well to do good," meaning that if you make a significant profit, then you can afford to support worthwhile nonprofit organizations. Nonprofits go to profit-making businesses to get their funding. Thus, good entrepreneurs make contributions to nonprofits to do good. *Entrepreneur* is also used in a more informal way to describe people with a sense of vision and innovation, which are key traits for anyone who wants to start their own profit-making business. A *serial entrepreneur* is someone who starts and runs several businesses, sometimes at the same time.

Starting a new business means that the company begins as a *small business*, which can be defined in various ways depending on the industry. Small businesses are privately owned enterprises set up as corporations, partnerships, or sole proprietorships that have less revenue and fewer employees than large businesses. The US Small Business Administration (SBA) uses complex formulas to determine what type of business qualifies as a small business. For example, a business in the wholesale trade segment with up to one hundred employees and $7 million in gross revenues is designated a small business, and a manufacturing entity of up to five hundred employees is considered a small business.

Entrepreneurship in the US and around the World

According to the SBA 2020 Small Business Profile, prior to the COVID-19 pandemic there were 31.7 million small profit-making businesses in the United States, representing 99.9 percent of US businesses, and 60.6 million small-business employees, representing 47 percent of total US employees.[1] In 2019, small businesses created 1.6 million net jobs, with firms with fewer than twenty employees representing the most job growth. While small businesses have been hit hard by the economic effects of the pandemic, they will play a key role in recovery for many years to come.[2] According to the World Bank, small- and medium-sized enterprises account for the majority of profit-making businesses worldwide, representing about 90 percent of businesses and more than 50 percent of employment.[3] The World Trade Organization's estimates are even higher, stating that small and medium enterprises account for 60 percent to 70 percent of global employment.[4]

---

1   2020 Small Business Profiles for the States and Territories," Office of Advocacy, Small Business Association, May 20, 2020, https://advocacy.sba.gov/2020/05/20/2020-small-business-profiles-for-the-states-and-territories/.

2   Sally Lauckner, "How Many Small Businesses Are in the US? (And Other Employment Stats)" Fundera by NerdWallet, updated September 9, 2020, https://www.fundera.com/blog/small-business-employment-and-growth-statistics.

3   "Small and Medium Enterprises (SMEs) Finance," World Bank, accessed January 2022, https://www.worldbank.org/en/topic/smefinance.

4   Christopher Arnold, "The Foundation for Economies Worldwide Is Small Business," IFAC.org, June 26, 2019, https://www.ifac.org/knowledge-gateway/contributing-global-economy/discussion/foundation-economies-worldwide-small-business-0.

What Motivates Entrepreneurs?

In 2018, marketing automation company HubSpot conducted a survey of its users, asking about their motivations for being entrepreneurs.[5] The top response (67 percent) was independence and more control of their destiny. More flexibility was a close second (66 percent), followed by a desire to make more money than in a salaried job (53 percent) and believing that they had a better chance for success as a business owner (47 percent). About a quarter of respondents (24 percent) said they were inspired by a successful entrepreneur they personally knew.

While this survey reflects some common reasons for starting a business, everyone's motivation is unique. The seed for a business idea can come from a desire to solve a specific problem or to pursue a passion. Stock media giant Shutterstock was founded by Jon Oringer in 2003 out of his frustration in using traditional stock image companies. Oringer was a serial entrepreneur, with ten companies under his belt before he hit on the concept for Shutterstock—a simplified process of licensing content images for use in marketing, websites, and publications. A software developer and amateur photographer, Oringer found a need and a successful way to fill it.

Why Start a Business While Still in College?

Starting a business while in college offers the chance to bypass the job-seeking stage and begin shaping the career you want right away. Instead of trying to fit into a corporate mold that may not be right for you, you can create a "job" that fits with your goals, priorities,

---

5   John Greathouse, "Of the 8 Top Reasons People Want to Be an Entrepreneur, 3 Are Sadly Lame," John Greathouse on Medium.com, November 27, 2018, https://medium.com/@johngreathouse/of-the-8-top-reasons-people-want-to-be-an-entrepreneur-3-are-sadly-lame-ba60d0c7c6fa.

dreams, and values. You don't have to wait until graduation for real life to begin.

Many colleges and universities offer a wide range of resources for student entrepreneurs. For example, the Lubar Entrepreneurship Center at the UWM (where I teach) offers an abundance of resources that include the following:

You don't have to wait until graduation for real life to begin.

- A place where courses are taught that integrate entrepreneurial thinking into the existing curriculum

- The Start-up Challenge, which encourages students to develop their ideas and launch businesses

- Innovation Talks, which are organized conversations with local entrepreneurs and innovators

- A variety of competitions in which students can earn cash prizes and seed capital

- An IT internship program

- The annual Innovators Expo

- A partnership in the Milwaukee I-Corps™ Program that links new venture and business mentors with academics toward the goal of commercializing research ideas

COLLEGIATE ENTREPRENEURS' ORGANIZATION

There is also the Collegiate Entrepreneurs' Organization (CEO), based in Tampa, Florida, which is an international entrepreneurship network with more than 250 chapters on university campuses in all fifty states and around the world. CEO works to inform, support, and inspire college students to seek opportunity through enterprise creation. The organization hosts programs, events, conferences, and chapter activities designed to help students start businesses. As a college student, you are encouraged to check out your local chapter or to start one if your college does not already have a chapter.

MENTORING PROGRAMS

Many schools offer mentoring programs in which experienced entrepreneurs counsel and work directly with students in the process of developing ideas and launching their businesses. These programs provide the opportunity for hands-on collaboration and are especially valuable for students without easy access to role models because none of their family members or friends own businesses. Mentors provide emotional support and real-world advice and guidance.

COMMUNITY AND GOVERNMENT RESOURCES

If you happen to be at a small school or one that doesn't offer a wide range of entrepreneurship resources, don't despair. Help and guidance are always available online and within your community. Two key organizations that offer assistance are SCORE and the SBA.

SCORE (https://www.score.org/) is a nonprofit organization that provides assistance through mentoring and education programs. They have the nation's largest network, more than ten thousand strong, of volunteers and expert business mentors who are available in local communities and via phone, email, and video conferencing. Services include mentoring, webinars, online resources, and local workshops and discussion groups. Most services are offered for free or at minimal cost.

The SBA offers a wealth of resources on their website (https://www.sba.gov/). This federal agency also offers free business counseling, SBA-guaranteed business loans, home and business disaster loans, and a certification program for small businesses interested in winning government contracts.

Learning the Entrepreneurial Ropes in College: One Student's Success Story

In 2017, a previous student at my university, Jesse DePinto, and his business partner Kyle Weatherly cofounded Frontdesk, Inc. (https://www.stayfrontdesk.com), a short-term rental company focused on providing unique guest experiences and comfortable, personalized stays for business and vacation travelers. Since then, Frontdesk has grown to host hundreds of suites in twenty-eight metropolitan areas, with more than 150 employees.

Here's Jesse's story of his path to success.

My parents weren't business owners—my mom was a teacher, and my dad was a machinist. But my dad was a first-generation immigrant from Italy, and he always had a kind of entrepreneurial spirit, coming to America for opportunity, so I think subconsciously he may have planted that seed for me.

Jesse DePinto

As a kid, when I was about ten or twelve years old, I shoveled snow and sold lemonade with a friend. We actually figured out that if we knocked on everybody's door and delivered the lemonade, we were more likely to get people to buy! When I was fourteen, my parents said it was time for me to start making money and sent me to work at an ice cream place for two hours a day, since that was the legal limit. That was good for my work ethic. I didn't do anything business related in high school. I was more of a nerd focused on my math and science classes.

It wasn't until college that I started my first business venture. I spent two years at Marquette and two years at the University of Wisconsin–Milwaukee majoring in engineering. When I was a sophomore at Marquette, I started my first business, producing and selling a tip-resistant hookah stand. I designed it on my CAD computer, manufactured it in India, and sold it through a distributor in California. While the business made only modest profits, it was satisfying to see that we could create and build a useful product that could be sold. After my second year at Marquette, I decided to transfer to the University of Wisconsin–Milwaukee to complete a degree in mechanical engineering.

At UWM, the innovation and commercialization and product realization courses were my most favorite classes I had ever taken in my life. UWM had just established the Student Startup Challenge, and with this support and funding I started a couple of businesses selling 3D printers and 3D printing services. I also won the La Macchia New Venture Business Plan Competition with a $10,000 prize.

I had a couple of partners in the business who came and went during the life of my business. One partner ended up being the cofounder and CEO of my current business, Frontdesk, LLC. It's important to make connections throughout your career, as you never know what partnerships might develop.

Our revenue from the 3D business was minimal, only $25,000, and my business partner and I lived very poorly for a year. During that time, I took advantage of all the UWM resources. The Collegiate Entrepreneurs' Organization was helpful. CEO mentors see entrepreneurship as a big economic driver, and they want to help each student succeed. I formed some of my deepest relationships that I still have today.

After graduation, I got married and took a job as a program manager in the aerospace industry to keep income coming in. I spent two years after that with a telecommunications firm, working on start-ups on the side. It took us nine months to get Frontdesk to the point where we had enough traction to pay myself a salary and quit my full-time job. We decided we had to turn a buck in month two, otherwise we wouldn't be able to dedicate our time to it. At the end of the day, it always comes back to cash in the bank.

It's important that you have people in your life who support your entrepreneurial spirit. I have an incredibly supportive wife. Here we are, ten years later. I have a paycheck, but she's still married to an entrepreneur, and that comes with its own challenges. Today, Frontdesk offers a more hotel-like experience than other rental options. We have self-check-in and other digital conventions and a great guest experience. It's a repeatable, predictable model. Kyle and I occupy two of seven board seats, and we have about ten investors, a combination of local family offices and venture capitalists.

I would do this forever just because I enjoy it. It's fun ... it's just fun. There's never an end to the challenges, and you learn so much and meet really cool people. Right now, the biggest thing is that there are 150-plus people counting on me, which is nerve racking but also a very rewarding experience. The culture we've created is now its own beast. It's wonderful; we have a lot of amazing people who are just good people and proud of the work they do.

Find something that's money making but also piques your interest. Chase traction and revenue instead of a business that may take years to show a profit.

Rewards and Challenges

Jesse's story illustrates the rewards of starting and running your own business. They include independence; the satisfaction of achieving something on your own (with help from mentors and associates), building a team, creating jobs and a positive work environment, and providing a useful product or service; and eventually financial rewards. Being a successful, profit-making business owner demands that you are constantly learning and growing.

On the flip side, there is no guarantee that your business will succeed. Jesse's first two businesses, though positive experiences, did not garner enough revenue for him to make a living. The uncertainty and ambiguity of entrepreneurship is the most challenging. Market conditions change, employees come and go, and new competitors emerge. Successful entrepreneurs face problems head on and are not afraid of a challenge. They are able to quickly size up a situation and make a decision. While there is no "magic formula" for success, there are certain personality traits and practical skills that successful business owners tend to have.

One of the most important things you can do when considering starting a business is to be honest with yourself. Can you see yourself as the head of an enterprise, making tough decisions when necessary? Is this vision of yourself what you really want? If you have clear goals and authentic and unrelenting drive and desire, you can make fantastic things happen, but can you remain true to who you really are? In chapter 2, we'll talk about personal traits, work habits, and essential skills that you'll need to forge your path as a collegiate entrepreneur.

Points to Remember

- ➡ An *entrepreneur* is a person who establishes and manages a new profit-making business, usually bearing all or most of the risks and benefiting from the rewards.

- ➡ Small businesses represent 99.9 percent of US businesses.

- ➡ Many colleges and universities offer a wide range of resources for student entrepreneurs, including courses, mentoring, specialized programs, conferences, and competitions.

- ➡ Community and government resources for budding entrepreneurs include SCORE and the SBA.

Recommended Resources

- ➡ Lubar Entrepreneurship Center:
  https://uwm.edu/lubar-entrepreneurship-center/

- ➡ The Collegiate Entrepreneurs' Organization: https://www.c-e-o.org/

- ➡ The SCORE Foundation: https://www.score.org/

- ➡ The US Small Business Administration: https://www.sba.gov/

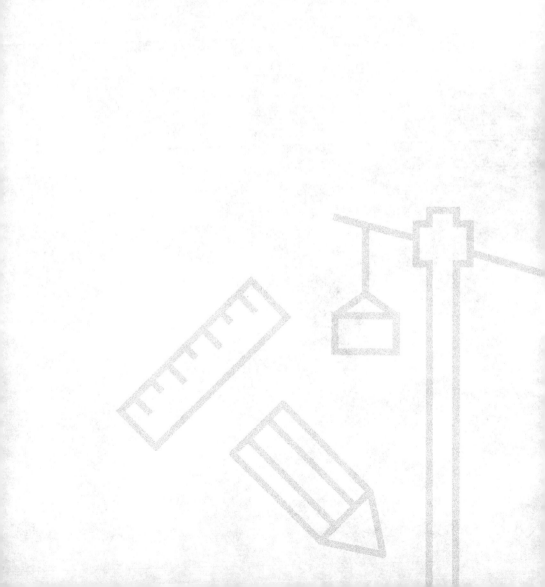

CHAPTER 2

DO YOU HAVE WHAT IT TAKES TO BE AN ENTREPRENEUR?

As a serious athlete, college student Caitie Gehlhausen had many of the same attributes as an entrepreneur: passion, perseverance, self-discipline, decisiveness, and resilience. Combining those strengths with a great idea and support from an entrepreneurial dad, Caitie had the courage to make the tough decision to give up playing Division I golf and go all in on her growing business.

From her first inkling of an idea to selling her Socket Lock-It™ smartphone accessory in Walmart, Caitie shares her story of success.

I pursued my dream of playing collegiate-level golf from the age of seven all the way through high school, so there wasn't much time for anything else. But because of the exposure that my dad provided through his own business, a research and development firm, there was always a part of me that was interested in starting a business. I took business classes in high school and participated in Business Professionals of America all four years. Once I started

Caitie Gehlhausen

college, I began to think more seriously about starting a business, but I struggled with coming up with any ideas of what that business would be.

My dad gave me a pep talk over the holiday break before I went back for my second semester, encouraging me to be highly observant of problems I was facing or that people around me were facing. He said that there are plenty of problems out there in the world that need solutions, and I needed to notice a legitimate problem and try to find a solution.

Amazingly, the first week I was back at school, I came across the problem I wanted to find a solution for. I was noticing that all my friends had either a grip or a cardholder on the back of their phone. A couple of people had tried to create a combination-type thing by gluing parts together, but it would fall apart after a few days. Students must have their ID with them all the time to get into campus buildings after hours and for meals and other things. One friend didn't want to lug around a purse or put her student ID and debit card in her pocket. She ended up losing them, and that was the spark for me to come up with the idea of the Socket Lock-It. I went online to try to find a gift for her, and to my surprise, there was nothing out there like what I was thinking of. That's when I went to my entrepreneurship professors and drew a couple of sketches of what I had in my head. I called my dad and told him I finally had a business idea. And that was just the beginning.

I played golf and worked on the business for about a year and a half. After my sophomore year, I realized that I needed to decide if I was really going to go all in on my business or if I'd hold back and continue trying to do both. I knew that I couldn't give 100 percent to both golf and my company, so I made the tough decision to hang up the sticks. But I'm super grateful for the experience of golfing, and I know I made the right decision. I graduated in three years, which allowed me to run the business full time.

My dad has always been my main mentor, and through him I came to understand that it's not all roses being an entrepreneur—but if you remain focused and persevere through the challenges, it can have a great payout in the end. I had two faculty mentors at High Point who were willing to share their knowledge in the start-up space. They were both committed to helping young entrepreneurs turn an idea into reality.

My school offered a lot of resources for entrepreneurship students, and I did a lot of extracurricular things. I participated in six pitch competitions and took advantage of every opportunity I had. I participated in the Collegiate Entrepreneurs' Organization (CEO) and did a pitch at that conference. All told, I raised $19,000 to put toward the business, and I needed every penny, because I had significant initial startup costs. The molds alone cost about $30,000 to have made. I had the molds made overseas, but we manufacture in the United States.

When COVID-19 hit, we had a bit of a setback. We didn't have enough going on for me to put in forty hours a week, so I accepted a sales position with a clothing manufacturer and retailer. And wouldn't you know, as soon as I accepted the position, I heard back from Walmart saying they wanted an interview with us.

More than fourteen thousand products are submitted each year to Walmart's open call program. They only accept 850 companies to interview with their buyers. And we were one of those selected. We pitched the product in October, and we got in! Several styles of Socket Lock-It are now sold in Walmart stores.

It was a lot of effort and determination to design and patent a product at the age of nineteen. I was fortunate to be able to launch the company and manufacture and sell a product while I was still in school. I honestly believe that one of the best times to start a business is in college, because people give you the benefit of the doubt when you're a student. There are a lot of people out there who truly want to help young entrepreneurs. As a student, you have access to a lot of free resources and support that you won't have once you graduate.

Today, Caitie runs the company with her mother and a team of freelance contractors. Socket Lock-It is sold direct to consumers and is also offered as a customized promotional product through B2B channels.

Are You Ready for Entrepreneurship?

When you begin dreaming about starting your own business, it's critical that you have a clear understanding of your strengths, weaknesses, and personality traits. You must be brutally honest with yourself to determine if entrepreneurship is the right choice. Take some time to do an honest assessment of your basic personality and current skills. Make a list of skills that you've mastered, at least to some degree, and another list of the knowledge and skills you'll need to develop or enhance to start and run your business. You don't have to be an expert in all areas, but you do need some basic competencies and the ability to find talented and trustworthy people to help you fill in the gaps.

A range of assessment tools is available online that can be used to help you evaluate your readiness for starting a business. These evaluate personal qualities, specific skills, and necessary knowledge for entrepreneurship. The SBA and SCORE both have similar assessments. The SBA online assessment tool may be found at https://eweb1.sba.gov/cams/training/business_primer/assessment.htm, and the SCORE Manasota of Sarasota, Florida, offers a downloadable PDF at https://manasota.score.org/resource/small-business-readiness-assessment-tool.

Essential Personal Characteristics of Entrepreneurs

In many ways, entrepreneurs are a separate breed. They have a much higher tolerance for risk than the average person and the drive and persistence that allows them to overcome obstacles that would stop others in their tracks. They are usually thought of as dreamers, but it's more than that—they're dreamers who figure out how to get things done. In the following sections, we'll review fourteen traits that are an essential part of the entrepreneurial personality. Do they describe you?

PASSION

Being passionate about a particular product, service, problem, or goal allows creativity to flow and great ideas to hatch. It also provides motivation when you're tired, overworked, and broke.

Apple cofounder Steve Jobs summed it up well:

You have to be burning with an idea, or a problem, or a wrong that you want to right. If you're not passionate enough from the start, you'll never stick it out.

Think about what's important to you. What kind of work life would excite you? What vision, problem, or goal holds your attention day and night? What kind of difference do you want to make in the world? For some people, their passion is already part of their everyday life, in the form of music, art, a sport, or a hobby. It could be a special talent such as baking cakes or inventing new gadgets or knowing how to design websites. But talent alone isn't enough—your passion has to get you excited and keep you excited, almost to the point of obsession.

If you have a lot of ideas, hobbies, or interests and aren't sure if any of them could truly be said to be your passion, it might be helpful to keep a journal for a couple of weeks or even longer. Each day, write down what had meaning for you that day, what made you happy or feel a sense of accomplishment or lose track of time. The process of unstructured writing can unblock the barriers put up by your rational mind and allow your most authentic thoughts and beliefs to emerge.

INTEGRITY AND HONESTY

Integrity can be defined as being honest and having strong moral principles. People with integrity are known for their decency and good character. In business, you may only have one chance to make a good impression on a vendor, potential employee, or potential customer. Acting with honesty and integrity is the basis for building solid business relationships. Famous author and motivational speaker Zig Ziglar said the following:

It is true that integrity alone won't make you a leader, but without integrity, you will never bc one.

SELF-DISCIPLINE

Self-discipline is the ability to motivate yourself, control your actions, and avoid distraction to stay on track to accomplish your goals. It involves setting clear, measurable goals and tracking your progress in achieving them. Self-discipline doesn't demand that you can't have any fun; it just means that you work when you need to work and play when it's time to play.

PERSEVERANCE

Perseverance is persistence in doing something despite challenges, difficulties, or delays in achieving success. When difficulties arise, people who persevere find their way through or around the difficulty while maintaining their focus and efforts on their next milestone or end goal.

OPTIMISM

Emotional intelligence is the ability to identify and understand your emotions and the emotions of others and the ability to manage your emotions. Optimism is a key part of emotional intelligence because it is an overall feeling of contentment and a generally positive outlook on life. It's a bias toward the positive, despite experiencing problems or hardship. Optimism comes more naturally to some people, but it is possible to cultivate it through gratitude and making a deliberate effort to focus on the positive aspects of any person or situation. For more on this topic, check out *Learned Optimism: How to Change Your Mind and Your Life*, by Martin E. P. Seligman.

SELF-CONFIDENCE

Self-confident people trust their own abilities and judgments and believe that they can successfully manage day-to-day challenges and demands. Self-confidence is not the same as arrogance, which is an exaggerated sense of one's abilities, worth, or importance. Self-confident people welcome input and ideas from other people.

FLEXIBILITY

Flexibility applies to both attitudes and actions. It involves open-mindedness and the ability to pivot (change course) on short notice. The ability to make adjustments in thinking and in actions in response to a changing environment is critical for entrepreneurs. Rigidly holding on to anything from the past—beliefs, methods, an organizational structure—in the face of changing circumstances is dangerous and can lead to business failure.

OPEN-MINDEDNESS

Open-mindedness is the willingness to consider ideas and opinions that differ from yours without prejudice or bias. No one can possibly know everything there is to know about any topic. The best leaders surround themselves with talented, knowledgeable people and genuinely listen to and consider their ideas and suggestions.

EMPATHY

Empathy is the ability to understand and be sensitive to the feelings of others. This trait is valuable in all aspects of personal and business interactions, paving the way for open and honest communication with business partners, employees, and customers, because you can picture yourself in their shoes and understand the challenges they may face. True leaders have empathy.

DECISIVENESS

Decisiveness is the ability to analyze information or a situation and make decisions quickly. This doesn't imply rash decision-making without considering possible effects and outcomes. This trait may not come easily to the scientifically or technically inclined who enjoy the process of analysis and problem solving. But sometimes acting too slowly or not acting at all can be costly. The ideal is to achieve a balance by obtaining all the necessary information in a timely manner and making the decision in time to bring about the desired result. It has been said that an entrepreneur makes decisions quickly *and* corrects wrong decisions quickly. Procrastination can be deadly!

CREATIVITY

People who are mechanically or technically inclined may think that creativity doesn't apply to their business. They think of creativity as an artistic ability such as being able to draw, paint, write, or compose music. While this sense of the word is correct, creativity encompasses much more. It's the ability to visualize, conceptualize, and "think outside the box" to find innovative solutions to problems.

ABILITY TO HANDLE UNCERTAINTY AND AMBIGUITY

A very important trait for anyone who wants to be an entrepreneur is being able to handle uncertainty and ambiguity. More often than not, the outcome of a given situation will not be known ahead of time. There will be frequent periods of uncertainty: You won't know if you'll get the loan. You won't know if the test run of your new product will be successful. You won't know if you've hired the right employees or spent your advertising budget on the right media or if the online reviews will be positive. Despite projections, you won't really know how long it will take to turn a profit. You must be able to weather this type of uncertainty while continuing to move forward. The uncertainty of entrepreneurship requires honest communication with a partner through all phases of business planning and operation.

RESILIENCE

Resilience has both a physical and a psychological aspect and is defined as the ability to withstand adversity and recover, to "bounce back" and move forward in spite of experiencing difficult life events. A healthy diet and exercise contribute to good health and the physical strength and stamina needed to work long hours. Emotional resilience is the ability to deal with difficulty and manage stress so it doesn't become debilitating. Each person has a unique set of coping skills, and it's important that you know what works for you. Whether it's making a midnight call to your best friend, going for a run, or meditating, you need to give yourself permission to engage in the type of self-care that works for you.

COURAGE TO ACT

We're all familiar with the Nike slogan "Just Do It." This directive is relevant for potential entrepreneurs because some people find it difficult to take action before they have every little detail planned out in advance. Planning is good, even great, but any plan only goes so far. Entrepreneurs must be able to "step out of the plane" with the confidence that their parachute will open. They must know when it's time to act and not be afraid to take the next step.

I've regretted saying it, but I once jokingly told a student who was taking forever to move forward with a reasonably well-thought-out plan, "Ready, fire, aim! Otherwise, you'll die before you take your first step." He took action, and it paid off, but he won't let me forget that somewhat ill-advised comment.

Assessing Your Skill Set

As you begin planning your business venture, it's a good idea to assess your current skills to determine which ones you currently possess and which will require further learning, formal training, or help from others. There's no right or wrong; the important thing is to end up with an honest picture of which aspects you can handle on your own and which skills you either need to learn or need to seek help from others to achieve. The following list represents skill areas to consider:

- Basic verbal and written communication skills, active listening skills

- People skills—the ability to develop positive relationships, supervise others, etc.

- Goal setting—the ability to set appropriate goals, work toward accomplishing them, and track progress

- Planning—the ability to make plans and track performance against the plan

- Money management—an understanding of financial/tax issues and basic accounting

- Networking—the ability to network to make contacts, get information, generate sales, etc.

- Negotiating skills—the ability to negotiate fair prices and terms for goods and services and to negotiate with employees and potential clients/customers

- Sales skills—the ability to convince people to buy your product or service

- Data-related skills—the ability to understand and interpret financial and other business-related data

What Specific Knowledge Do You Need?

No matter what type of business you want to start, you need a certain amount of knowledge related to the specific product or service that you'll offer. Who are your competitors? How are their products or services priced, marketed, and delivered? Who's your target market, and how will you reach them? How will you manufacture or ship your product in a timely and cost-effective way? In the chapters that follow, we'll outline the processes involved in researching, planning, funding, and ultimately launching your new business.

An ideal way to gain knowledge is to spend at least two months working in every functional area of a business.

An ideal way to gain knowledge is to spend at least two months working in every functional area of a business. Functional areas may include the following:

- Human Resources
- Accounting/finance
- Purchasing
- Legal
- Administration/management
- Information technology
- Research and development
- Production
- Operations
- Distribution
- Marketing and promotion
- Sales
- Customer service

This type of experiential learning is an important supplement to "book learning." While your classroom experience will provide a great deal of useful knowledge, real-world experience is invaluable. You can seek out internships, part-time work, volunteer gigs, and site visits to provide exposure to various functional areas. Talking with mentors and other business owners can also help you fill in the blanks.

Entrepreneurs often find accounting to be challenging or uninteresting, but every business owner *must know* where the company stands financially as a basis for decision-making, and that is only possible if they have knowledge of basic accounting. A partner, advisor, or employee with strong financial skills can provide information and possibly be tasked with day-to-day financial management, but every owner must understand what the numbers mean.

Points to Remember

➡ Develop a clear understanding of your strengths, weaknesses, and personality traits to determine if entrepreneurship is the right choice for you.

➡ Assess your current skill set to determine which skills you currently possess and which will require further learning, formal training, or help from others.

➡ Essential skills for business owners include verbal and written communication, people skills, goal setting, planning, basic accounting and money management, networking, negotiating, sales, and data-related skills.

➡ Gain industry-specific knowledge via internships, part-time work, volunteer gigs, and site visits that offer exposure to various functional areas. Talking with mentors and other business owners can also provide helpful information.

Recommended Resources:

➡ *Learned Optimism: How to Change Your Mind and Your Life*, by Martin E. P. Seligman.

➡ *The College Entrepreneur*, by Kyle Gray

CHAPTER 3

VISUALIZING AND TESTING YOUR BIG IDEA

Jared Judge is no stranger to visualizing big ideas and turning them into businesses. At thirteen, he taught himself code as a hobby and the following year signed up with a freelancing website and acquired a client who hired him to develop a basic hotel room reservation system for his property in Aruba. In high school, he founded the African Drum Circle Club, writing a successful grant proposal to acquire several authentic drums. Jared's ability to visualize ideas and his willingness to test them out has led to his continued entrepreneurial success.

I completed my bachelor's degree in music education at Penn State and moved to New Jersey to teach music in a public school. I wanted to find an opportunity to continue playing music (violin and viola), not just teaching it, so I got involved with a local opera company, performing and acting as a volunteer assistant to the director. At the end of the season, the director left. The staff, singers, and musicians were all disappointed, so I volunteered to step up and take over. The company had been sponsored by another organization, so I reinvented it as a 501(c)(3) nonprofit. That's when I decided to upgrade the website so people could purchase tickets online. I learned how to network with donors and convey the value we were bringing to the community. I raised about $15,000 for the season and obtained

Jared Judge (foreground)

a couple of corporate sponsorships. Our first season as a nonprofit was a success. It also turned out to be my last season, as I'd been accepted for graduate study at the University of Wisconsin–Milwaukee (UWM).

Halfway through my first year of grad school, I got the idea for Dream City Strings (now part of Dream City Music). Money was getting tight, and I was working at a job that took up a lot of time but had nothing to do with my passion. I decided to start my own company, create a great website, and play my instrument—something I love to do—and get paid for it. Once I had the idea, there was no turning back.

I was fortunate to be immersed at UWM and to have been able to reach out to the business school. I received help from people at the Lubar Entrepreneurship Center related to the business aspects of booking. In my second year, I came across the Collegiate Entrepreneurs' Organization (CEO) and went to the CEO Global Conference in Tampa. I became involved in other UWM programs such as the Ideas Challenge and Student Startup Challenge. I also participated in an eight-week entrepreneurship program offered by The Commons, a local nonprofit.

Dream City Strings officially started in March 2016. We started to get bookings, and I decided, *OK, this is a real business, and it's time to take it seriously*. I registered the LLC and established structures, procedures, and systems. In 2018, I established BookLive, a website that simplifies the process of selecting and booking live entertainment for clients planning weddings and other special events in the Milwaukee and Chicago areas. There are a couple of competitors in the area, but we provide what they don't. Our competitors simply facilitate a connection, we go way beyond that and help the artists price their services and conduct business. This was important to me because most musicians don't have a degree in business. They want to make a living with music, but they just don't know how—BookLive solves that problem for them.

Where Do the Ideas Come From?

The key to a successful business idea for Jared came from pursuing his passion for playing music and solving a problem for fellow musicians.

For Josh Shefner, founder and CEO of Agricycle Global, his entrepreneurial idea came from his passion for bringing people together who share a common interest and motivating them to act as well as his desire to create a solution to reduce food waste and help rural communities.

I wasn't into any type of entrepreneurial activity as a kid. I was more about bringing people together who shared a common interest and motivating them to take action. In

high school, I started an academic competitions team. I was part of the honors program in college, and one of my year-long projects ended up being incredibly entrepreneurial. It's where I got the idea for what I'm doing now.

Josh Shefner

The honors project they came to us with was a nonprofit in Jamaica that said, "Hey, mangoes grow crazy out here. We need to do something with the mangoes. We've tried jamming them, we've tried juicing them, we're going to try drying them, and now we're going to take dried mangoes and turn them into beer. We need you." We needed to figure out a business model for turning dried mangoes into beer. It was a terrible idea. We went to the National Science Foundation's Innovation Corps for a four- or five-week program and very quickly pivoted to selling dried fruits.

We joined The Commons, which helped accelerate our idea of producing dried mangoes. A design team from the University of Michigan was supposed to design the dehydrator, but they dropped out. So, our group of MSOE freshmen ended up designing a solar-powered dehydrator. We traveled to Jamaica and built a dehydrator there successfully.

To make a long story short, all didn't go as planned in terms of working with local organizations in Jamaica, so we weren't able to move forward there. But the basic business idea was formulated and piloted, and I took it in a different direction with a focus on reducing food waste in rural communities.

At Agricycle, we no longer work through nonprofits; we have local staff and work directly with communities and farmers. We got into the Target Incubator, which was a program for start-ups that included workshops and mentorship sessions. Soon after, we raised over $1 million from angel investors and a venture capital firm.

The majority of food that goes to waste before it can go to market is from small farms. We provide the simple technology that in turn provides a saleable food product. We design machines that work without electricity, sell them to farmers and others in rural communities, and train them how to use the machines. And then we purchase the products they make using our machines and sell them to consumers and wholesalers in the US.

> We're continuing to have a positive impact on small farmers, rural communities, and the environment. We're expanding in Africa and Latin America, and we're partnering to provide clean water, solar power, electricity, and healthcare to members of our network.
>
> I get the most satisfaction from knowing that I've created jobs and helped improve people's lives.

There is no "perfect" or "sure-fire" business idea, only the one that is right for you and right for the market at a given point in time. Potential entrepreneurs come up with business ideas in a wide variety of ways. In this section, we'll take a look at some common approaches when starting from scratch to identify a customer problem to solve.

There is no "perfect" or "sure-fire" business idea, only the one that is right for you and right for the market at a given point in time.

OBSERVATION

Many business ideas emerge from observing others experiencing some type of problem. As Caitie described, she watched her friends attach a phone grip or cardholder to the back of their phones. She saw some attempting to cobble together a combination device by gluing the pieces together. Those observations were the spark for her solution, which became the Socket Lock-It.

If you haven't yet landed on a business idea that resonates with you, make an effort to slow down and pay more attention to people around you. Listen carefully when they describe things that have been a difficult or frustrating part of their day. Make notes and track if certain problems crop up repeatedly or are mentioned by more than just a few people. Be sure to talk with a wide range of people to include those of different ages and from various backgrounds and occupations.

PERSONAL EXPERIENCE

Often a business idea emerges from a problem you experience yourself. For example, former fashion stylist Irene Agbontaen is five foot eleven and had many frustrating experiences trying to find attractive clothing that fit properly. In 2013, she founded TTYA London (Taller Than Your Average), a line of women's apparel that focuses on well-fitting, elegant, functional clothing for women who are five foot nine or taller. Today, her collection is sold online and in upscale department stores in the US and UK. Irene's business concept addressed a legitimate problem and offered a viable, appealing solution for tall women.

PURSUING A PASSION OR MISSION

Jared's passion for music led to his founding not one, but two companies. Josh's mission to reduce food waste and help rural communities has led to the creation of nearly sixty-eight hundred livelihoods across the globe. If you have a special talent, skill, or hobby that you love, consider how it might translate into a profitable business. You may think that this pathway only applies to creative types such as musicians, artists, and craftspeople, but it can emerge from other skill sets as well. Tech types have established all kinds of businesses, from software development to web design to cybersecurity. People with a knack for planning and organizing start event planning companies and home- and business-organizing services. Number crunchers start accounting, financial planning, and investment firms. Animal lovers start pet-sitting, grooming, and dog-walking services.

RESEARCH

If personal experience and the experiences of those you know aren't "bubbling up" any business ideas, it may be time to do some research. Some resources are listed at the end of the chapter that might help with ideas and inspiration. But first, below is my list of thirty-five business ideas for college students:

1. Laundry service for students who are too busy or dislike doing laundry (picking up, washing/drying, folding, and delivery)

2. Package delivery service

3. Food delivery service

4. House-sitting services

5. Home or appliance repair

6. Home maintenance services such as lawn care, snow removal, gutter cleaning

7. Home painting or wallpapering services

8. Childcare or senior care services

9. Transportation services for the elderly and others who don't drive

10. Dog-walking, pet-sitting, and/or pet-grooming services

11. Health coaching services

12. Personal training services

13. Tutoring services for classes for which you have expertise

14. Tour guiding for visitors to your area

15. Virtual assistant to provide administrative or tech services

16. Social media consultant to help others promote their products/services

17. Website development services

18. App development

19. Video creation services

20. DJ services

21. Editing services for college students and members of the college community

22. Résumé writing or editing services

23. Illustration services for writers and others needing illustrations or graphics

24. Create and sell art, jewelry, clothing, or craft items

25. Create and sell custom T-shirts

26. Find a unique product (ideally made inexpensively overseas) and sell on campus and beyond

27. Find or create products to sell at a local flea market or farmer's market

28. Sell items from garage, yard, and estate sales online on eBay and/or other sales sites

29. Write and sell e-books on Amazon.com

30. Buy and sell used textbooks directly and online

31. Become a podcaster or blogger on a topic of interest, and generate revenue via advertising, sponsorships, and affiliation programs

32. Create and sell a welcome kit with "insider tips" for incoming freshmen

33. Start a student magazine, and generate revenue via subscriptions and advertising

34. Musicians: perform at home and business events

35. Invent a brand-new product, patent it, and sell or license it

The IDEATE Method

Ideation is the process of forming ideas or images in the mind. The IDEATE Method[6] is an ideation method that has demonstrated success in helping students identify problems, develop creative solutions, and select the most innovative entrepreneurial ideas to pursue. The method has been summarized in workbook format (see "Recommended Resources" at the end of the chapter), and I encourage you to read the workbook and complete the exercises as part of your business development activities. The following sections outline the key steps that make up the IDEATE process:

I—Identify Problems and Potential Solutions

Learn to recognize what makes a potential business idea valuable. The goal at this point is to identify what the authors call "migraine headache" problems that are worth solving. Once real problems are identified, the idea generation process can begin. You look at the root cause of each problem and consider possible solutions. At this stage, you are learning to differentiate between ideas that are valuable versus those that are not worth the time, effort, or money to pursue.

D—Discover Areas of Opportunity

---

6   Dan Cohen, Greg Pool, and Heidi Neck, *The IDEATE Method: Identifying High-Potential Entrepreneurial Ideas* (Los Angeles: SAGE Publications, Inc. 2021).

Actively search for opportunities in problem-rich environments. The challenge is to discover at least ten ideas based on your personal experiences of daily life, expertise or talents you have, activities you're passionate about, and business ideas or current trends that seem to be gaining traction in the marketplace.

E—Enhance Existing Ideas

Look for ways to enhance an opportunity in an innovative way to create more value. This stage focuses on ways to turn smaller ideas into bigger, bolder ideas and to tweak ideas to reach their fullest potential.

A—Anticipate Change

All types of change can be a source of opportunity. Think about social and demographic changes, technological changes, industry and market changes, and political and regulatory changes. Once real or potential changes are identified, it's possible to visualize opportunities that may emerge from these changes.

T—Target the Market

Focus on identifying your target market for each potential idea and learning as much as you can about potential customers. Once you have a solid understanding of the target market, you then investigate what other needs these potential customers may have, which will lead to refinements in your product or service and ideas for additional products or services.

E—Evaluate Your Business Ideas

Now that you have more than a handful of business ideas that you believe are viable, it's time to get tough and evaluate each one based on both personal and market-based criteria. Look at

- the size of the problem and potential market, and determine if enough people are willing to pay for your solution to make a business profitable;

- how well the business proposition fits with your skills, experience, lifestyle, and resources; and

- whether your product or service really does offer something new or an improvement over current products or services.

You'll make an honest assessment of your enthusiasm (or lack of enthusiasm) for pursuing this idea. At the end of this stage, you'll have at least one valuable business idea (hopefully more) with high potential for success.

Choose Your Best Idea and Create a Business Model Canvas

The savvy entrepreneur needs both a business model canvas and a business plan. What's the difference? A *business model* canvas is a one-page rationale and framework for how a business will make a profit. Creating a canvas for your best idea is the next step in the process. The *business plan* (discussed in detail in chapter 6) comes later in the process and is a written description of the business concept and the resources and steps needed to launch the business and make it successful.

THE BUSINESS MODEL CANVAS

The Business Model Canvas was developed by Alexander Osterwalder and Yves Pigneur in 2004. Their best-selling book, *Business Model Generation*, published in 2010 by Wiley, introduced the concept as a planning and management tool. The canvas template has been published online under a Creative Commons license (https://www. strategyzer.com/canvas/business-model-canvas) and is available for use by students and entrepreneurs.

BUILDING BLOCKS

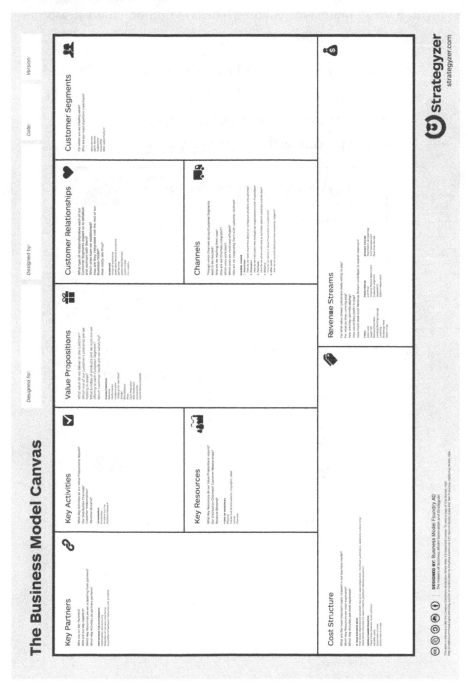

Figure 3.1: Osterwalder's Business Model Canvas

The canvas is usually created very early in a venture's development. It incorporates nine building blocks to outline almost all aspects of a new business (figure 3.1):

1. **Customer Segments:** Who are the customers? What do they think, see, feel, and do? Which customer segments are likely to provide the most revenue? How would you describe your archetypal customer (age, income, interests, etc.)?

Customer Segments

For whom are we creating value?
Who are our most important customers?

Mass market
Niche market
Segmented
Diversified
Multi-sided platform

2. **Value Propositions:** What are your products/services? What value do you bring to the customer? What is unique or compelling about the value propositions? Why will customers buy or use this product or service?

Value Propositions

What value do we deliver to the customer?
Which one of our customers' problems are we helping to solve?
What bundles of products and services are we offering to each Customer Segment?
Which customer needs are we satisfying?

CHARACTERISTICS
Newness
Performance
Customization
"Getting the Job Done"
Design
Brand/status
Price
Cost reduction
Risk reduction
Accessibility
Convenience/usability

3. **Channels:** How will you reach the customer and gain the sale? How will you deliver the value proposition (product/service)?

Channels

Through which Channels do our Customer Segments want to be reached?
How are we reaching them now?
How are our Channels integrated?
Which ones work best?
Which ones are most cost-efficient?
How are we integrating them with customer routines?

CHANNEL PHASES
1. *Awareness*
   How do we raise awareness about our company's products and services?
2. *Evaluation*
   How do we help customers evaluate our organization's Value Proposition?
3. *Purchase*
   How do we allow customers to purchase specific products and services?
4. *Delivery*
   How do we deliver a Value Proposition to customers?
5. *After sales*
   How do we provide post-purchase customer support?

4. **Customer Relationships:** How will you establish and maintain your relationship with the customer? How will the company/team support customers and keep in touch with their needs?

Customer Relationships

What type of relationship does each of our Customer Segments expect us to establish and maintain with them?
Which ones have we established?
How are they integrated with the rest of our business model?
How costly are they?

EXAMPLES
Personal assistance
Dedicated personal assistance
Self-Service
Automated services
Communities
Co-creation

5. **Revenue Streams:** How will the product/service make money? A revenue stream could be a payment for a(n)

    a. event or product,

    b. period of time that the customer enjoys/uses the product/service,

    c. promotional services (advertising), or

    d. rental or sale of a product or service.

Revenue Streams

For what value are our customers really willing to pay?
For what do they currently pay?
How are they currently paying?
How would they prefer to pay?
How much does each Revenue Stream contribute to overall revenues?

TYPES	FIXED PRICING	DYNAMIC PRICING
Asset sale	*List price*	*Negotiation (bargaining)*
Usage fee	*Product feature dependent*	*Yield management*
Subscription fees	*Customer segment*	*Real-time-market*
Lending/renting/leasing	*dependent*	
Licensing	*Volume dependent*	
Brokerage fees		
Advertising		

---

6. **Key Resources:** Who are the key people you need to run the business? What financial resources, assets, knowledge, and tools are needed to be competitive in the marketplace?

Key Resources

What Key Resources do our Value Propositions require?
Our Distribution Channels? Customer Relationships?
Revenue Streams?

TYPES OF RESOURCES
Physical
Intellectual (brand patents, copyrights, data)
Human
Financial

---

7. **Key Activities:** What steps must be completed to make the enterprise a success? What strategic actions must the business take to deliver its value proposition? What must be done on a day-to-day basis to run the business?

Key Activities

What Key Activities do our Value Propositions require?
Our Distribution Channels?
Customer Relationships?
Revenue Streams

CATERGORIES
Production
Problem Solving
Platform/network

8. **Key Partnerships:** What partners are needed to make the business successful? An entrepreneur usually cannot perform all functions of a complete business. So, a key partner could be an individual or organization that performs an important function for the business that the entrepreneur decides to "farm out."

Key Partners

Who are our Key Partners?
Who are our Key Suppliers?
Which Key Resources are we acquairing from partners?
Which Key Activities do partners perform?

MOTIVATIONS FOR PARTNERSHIPS
Optimization and economy
Reduction of risk and uncertainty
Acquisition of particular resources and activities

9. **Cost Structure:** Based on anticipated activities and available resources, what does it cost to create the product/service and sell and support it?

Cost Structure

What are the most important costs inherent in our business model?
Which Key Resources are most expensive?
Which Key Activities are most expensive?

IS YOUR BUSINESS MORE...
Cost-driven (leanest cost structure, low price value proposition, maximum automation, extensive outsourcing)
Value-driven (focused on value creation, premium value proposition)

SAMPLE CHARACTERISTICS
Fixed costs (salaries, rents, utilities)
Variable costs
Economies of scale
Economies of scope

HOW TO USE THE CANVAS

The entrepreneur (often with the help of a select team of partners, advisors, and/or mentors) addresses each of these building blocks and makes educated guesses as to the nature of activities to be conducted in each area. It's important to assemble the right team for this activity and allow at least forty-five minutes to an hour of uninterrupted time to work on it. If more research or discussion with team members is needed, complete as much as you can during your first session and set a time to regroup and continue the process. This initial draft is just a set of "educated guesses" as you fill out the nine building blocks. It is important to be as comprehensive as possible, but don't get hung up in any particular area of the canvas because the initial canvas consists of just "best guesses." You will convert these guesses into "facts" as you conduct customer discovery (discussed in chapter 4). Working on the canvas pushes the entrepreneur to think about all major elements of the business and to create and test hypotheses, which will change as facts emerge.

Once the first draft of the canvas has been created, the entrepreneur engages in customer discovery to prove, disprove, and revise the assumptions made in the initial canvas. As the process of customer discovery brings new information to light, the canvas can easily be revised to reflect updated knowledge that may challenge previous assumptions. This process of creating a Business Model Canvas, performing customer discovery, and updating the canvas has saved entrepreneurs thousands and sometimes even millions of dollars that would have otherwise been spent based on an unproven set of assumptions.

You can also run your idea through the Opportunity Checklist first published in *Entrepreneurship*, by Zacharakis, Corbett, and Bygrave. A copy of this checklist may be found in this book's appendices.[7]

Once you're 100 percent committed to your business idea, you need a plan. In chapter 6, we'll walk through creating a business plan that includes all the essential elements you'll need to transform your idea from concept to reality. But first things first: it's time to dive into the art of customer discovery.

Points to Remember

- ➡ The key to a successful business idea is solving a customer problem.

- ➡ Common approaches used to identify a customer problem to solve include personal experience, observation of problems in daily life, research, and pursuing a passion or mission.

- ➡ Once customer feedback has been gathered and analyzed, a final value check, risk check, and gut check will help ensure that you've created a solid business idea.

---

7   A. Zacharakis, A. Corbett, and W. Bygrave, *Entrepreneurship*, 5th Edition (New York: Wiley, 2020).

Recommended Resources

- ➡ *The IDEATE Method*, by Dan Cohen, Greg Pool, and Heidi Neck

- ➡ Business Model Generation: A Handbook for Visionaries, Game Changers, and Challengers, by Alexander Osterwalder and Yves Pigneur

- ➡ *Entrepreneurship*, by Zacharakis, Corbett, and Bygrave

- ➡ *Entrepreneurship: The Practice and Mindset*, by Heidi M. Neck, Christopher P. Neck, and Emma L. Murray.

The following links are to articles that offer business ideas for college students:

- "How to Make Money in Business with a Side Hustle": https://sba.thehartford.com/finance/ideas-small-businesses-make-money/

- "145 New Service Business Ideas for 2022": https://www.nerdwallet.com/article/small-business/service-business-ideas

- "53 Small Business Ideas to Start at University": https://www.savethestudent.org/make-money/50-business-ideas-to-start-at-university.html

- "50 Business Ideas for College Students": https://smallbiztrends.com/2016/12/business-ideas-for-college-students.html

- "52 Student Business Ideas and Startup Opportunities": https://entrepreneurhandbook.co.uk/student-business-ideas/

CHAPTER 4

CUSTOMER DISCOVERY

How many times do you snack per day? When did you last have fruit for a snack?

These were just two of the questions that Matt Kemper, a student entrepreneur, needed answers to as he began his customer discovery process for his first professional business venture. By the time Matt entered college, inklings of entrepreneurship had already begun.

I'm the youngest of nine kids, and so there wasn't really money to go around. If you wanted something, you had to go work for it. I started mowing lawns in sixth grade to pay for things that I wanted, but I also just enjoyed it. I loved working for myself and being in control of the customer experience.

Matt Kemper

My work was good, my customers were happy, and the business just grew. Building a loyal customer base was addicting to me.

In high school, I started working at Dairy Queen, and I worked in several restaurants through my sophomore year in college. I really enjoyed working for small business owners and learning about different aspects of the business. By my senior year in high school, I was managing a local ice cream shop.

In my freshman year in college, I joined the Collegiate Entrepreneurs' Organization at the University of Wisconsin–Milwaukee. Part of the program involved listening to the elevator pitches of fellow students. One of those pitches was for a company called Light Fruit Company, which created crispy and tasty watermelon chips from dehydrated watermelon. At the final CEO meeting of my freshman year, James, the founder of Light Fruit Company, said to me, "I'm a geology student, and I need a business student to be cofounder in order to enter a business plan competition. Are you interested?"

I said yes, and we went to work developing a detailed business plan and preparing for the competition. We won the competition and were awarded $5,000 in seed funding. We went on to enter a competition run by a local radio station and won an additional $10,000 award.

The Light Fruit Company was on a roll!

What was the secret to their success? It wasn't just about the crispy, tasty watermelon chips—the end product is just one component of the equation, after all. The competitions also required proof of the chips' attractiveness to potential customers. Matt and his partner found their proof through the *customer discovery process*.

Customer Discovery: What's It All About?

The goal of customer discovery is to test a founder's hypotheses and assumptions about their market and customers in order to prove which ones are based in fact. Steve Blank, author of *The Startup Owner's Manual* and *The Four Steps to the Epiphany*, identifies four key questions that are the foundation on which to launch the customer discovery process. At the end of the process, a founder should have clear answers to the following:

1. Have we identified a problem a customer wants to see solved?

2. Does our product/service solve this customer problem or need?

3. If so, do we have a viable and profitable business model?

4. Have we learned enough to go out and sell?

Now, the question is this: How do you go about getting answers to these questions?

Here is what Steve Blank, author and retired Stanford professor, says about using his Lean LaunchPad model: "The Lean LaunchPad is built around the business model / customer development / agile development solution stack. Students start by mapping their initial assumptions (their business model). Each week they test these hypotheses with customers and partners outside the classroom (using customer development), then use iterative and incremental development (agile development) to build minimal viable products. The goal is to get students out of the building to test each of the nine components of their Business Model Canvas, understand which of their assumptions were wrong, and figure out what they need to do to find product/market fit and develop a validated business model."

Armed with your hypotheses, it's time to venture out into the real world to test your assumptions about your potential customers' pain points, how to solve them, and which are valid. Yes, you will have to find and talk to potential customers!

Steve recommends creating an initial list of fifty people to reach out to and schedule a time to interview. Now, you may not be able to list fifty people at one time, but begin with those you know who, on some level, fit your customer hypotheses (friends, family, coworkers, classmates) and build from there. Ask those initial contacts to refer you to their friends, family, and coworkers—social media platforms can be a useful tool in quickly making those connections. Use social media to help create your list of people to contact. The customer discovery process is to be person to person.

Do research on those you are calling on, make a list of questions in advance of your first interviews, schedule the interviews, and then prepare to really listen. It's critical to remember that at this juncture, the goal is *not* to sell anyone anything; the goal is to garner information (listen intently and create follow-up questions based on their feedback) that helps you understand your customers' actual needs and how they might be solved, *even if their answers contradict your assumptions.* As you speak to more potential customers, your list of questions should change, reflecting the information you have garnered from previous interviews. In this phase, you are looking for a small group of individuals ("earlyvangelists," as Steve Blank calls them) who clearly confirm that they have the problem you are offering a solution to—they have tried to solve the problem but are still floundering, they have a budget for solving the problem, and they display a passion for your product.

It's critical through this process that you are open to disinterest in and lack of need for your product. This is information that you will use to reexamine who you thought your customers were *and* the possibility that customers may not exist for your product, at which point, based on those results, it's time to determine whether you should pivot or persevere. It's better to learn and accept at the customer discovery stage that your business is not viable rather than after you have invested years of time and money trying to convince people that they need your product.

It's better to learn and accept at the customer discovery stage that your business is not viable rather than after you have invested years of time and money trying to convince people that they need your product.

The Mom Test

While an ardent believer in the customer discovery process, Rob Fitzpatrick, author of *The Mom Test*, encourages a more causal and informal approach to asking questions in the wild. Fitzpatrick recommends that, in the initial phase of questioning, the customer being questioned should be unaware that you are researching a potential product. Instead, it should be an impromptu, casual line of questioning about what you see as a struggle or interest for them, setting the stage for objective, factual answers rather than opinions and compliments. Here is an example from *The Mom Test:*[8]

---

8   Rob Fitzpatrick, The Mom Test: How to Talk to Customers and Learn if Your Business Is a Good Idea When Everyone Is Lying to You (Scotts Valley, California: CreateSpace, September 10, 2013).

Son: "Mom, I have an idea for a business. Can I run it by you?"
Mom: "Of course, dear."
Son: "You like your iPad, right? You use it a lot?"
Mom: "Yes."
Son: "Okay, so would you ever buy an app that was like a cookbook for your iPad?"
Mom: "Hmmm."

You can see where this is going. In the end, most moms are going to say, "That's brilliant—of course I'll buy one!" regardless of how useful they think it really is. Here's Rob's recommended alternate approach:[9]

Son: "Hey, Mom, how's that new iPad treating you?"
Mom: "Oh—I love it! I use it every day."
Son: "What's the last thing you did on it?"
Mom: "You know your father and I are planning that trip. I was figuring out where we could stay."
Son: "Did you use an app for that?"
Mom: "No, I just used Google. I didn't know there was an app."
Son: "How did you find out about the other apps you have?"
Mom: "The Sunday paper has a section on the apps of the week."
Son: "Makes sense. By the way, I saw a couple of cookbooks on the shelf—where did those come from?"
Mom: "They're some of those things people keep giving you. I think Marcy gave me that last one. Haven't even opened it. As if I need another lasagna recipe at my age."
Son: "What's the last cookbook you did buy for yourself?"
Mom: "I bought a vegan cookbook about three months ago. Your father is trying to eat healthier."

---

9   Ibid.

The second approach garnered a lot more useful *and factual* information, and it was all done without leading the mom to the answer the son wanted or making the mom feel compelled to lie so as not to hurt her son's feelings—it passed the mom test. You can also see how the son created his follow-up questions in line with his mom's answers, continuing to clarify whether or not it was a product she would use. He could have walked away when she responded that cookbooks are some of the things people keep giving her and she doesn't even open, but he continued to dig and discovered that there might be potential after all.

This type of informal questioning can be done with all types of potential customers— family, friends, coworkers, classmates. The goal is to gather objective information (facts, not opinions) from forty to fifty potential customers, gaining information about their past experiences and how they imagine the experience could have been better. This can be accomplished by asking questions based on the customer's life and behaviors.

Matt and his cofounder followed this approach after reading *The Mom Test*. Here are more of the questions they asked:

- How many times today did you snack?

- When did you last have fruit for a snack? What fruit was it?

- If you had a fruit snack, what was the snack?

- If your snack contained fruit, what quantity of fruit was in the snack?

- In the past two weeks, what quantity of fruit did you have as a snack?

- If your snack was a package snack (any kind of snack), what was the quantity in the package (ounces)? Was that quantity sufficient?

- What was the shelf life of a snack that you bought? Describe.

- Were any of your snacks purchased dehydrated fruit? Describe.

- Where did you buy your snacks? List all.

- What did you pay for the snacks that you purchased recently? What did you buy? Describe what the snack was and the quantity purchased for the price paid.

- What is your reaction to the snack provided as a sample? Taste? Quantity per package? Appearance?

As you can see from Matt's questions, the goal is to ask questions that reveal information about the customer's life, needs, and problems and not what the entrepreneur should build, create, or sell. Listen carefully. The information they gathered from their fifty customer discovery interviews convinced them, as well as those who reviewed their business plan, that the Light Fruit Company could be a viable business.

In addition to an overall positive response, Matt and his team learned additional valuable insights:

> *The goal is to ask questions that reveal information about the customer's life, needs, and problems and not what the entrepreneur should build, create, or sell. Listen carefully.*

- A one-ounce bag was preferable to a half-ounce bag.

- A snack could last two to five hours as a customer slowly enjoyed the snack.

- A customer wants to know what the shelf life of a snack would be, as they might buy a snack and store it in a cupboard for weeks.

- Customers might buy this kind of snack at a farmers' market, at Beans & Barley, or around campus, such as at the University of Wisconsin–Milwaukee.

- Customers had never tried dehydrated watermelon before.

- None of the students interviewed reported having eaten two servings of fruit per day in the past week. The students reported that they didn't eat fruit due to cost and convenience issues.

- Customers reported that accessibility and convenience are the primary influencing factors in snack choice.

- Customers reported that a mass-market dehydrated melon is not presently available to the consumer in single-serving sizes.

- There are no dehydrated watermelon, cantaloupe, and honeydew products available to consumers in the greater Milwaukee area.

Questions such as "What have you tried so far?" and "What are the implications of that?" encourage the customer to elaborate and provide more details. The question "Is there anything else I should have asked?" near the end of the meeting opens the door for the customer to provide information you may not have thought to ask about. Asking "Who else should I talk to?" can lead you to other potential customers who may offer helpful insights. It's important to take notes and record the interviews. After you've gathered as much specific information as possible, then it's your job to analyze the feedback and move into the *customer validation* phase.

Customer Validation

Once you have collected your data and completed the initial phase of the customer discovery process, you're ready to validate your findings.

With the information from your interviews, you adapt your hypotheses accordingly and make iterative adjustments to your product. The focus is on preparing your product for sale to the small group of earlyvangelists you have begun to form a relationship with. The intent is not to adapt your product (every imaginable feature, lots of "nice-to-haves") to meet mainstream consumption. This is the time to incorporate only your must-haves for your initial group of customers and prepare to sell to them.

Blank outlines the preparation for a company's first attempt at selling its product:[10]

- Articulate a value proposition: The value a company promises to deliver to customers should they choose to buy their product (remember the elevator pitch from chapter 4?).

- Prepare sales materials and initial collateral plan: Using your value proposition, create *preliminary* (low-volume and low-cost) product data sheets, sales materials, and presentations.

- Develop a *preliminary* distribution channel plan: Create a road map of how you will most effectively get your product into the hands of your end users.

- Develop a *preliminary* sales road map: You know who your end users are, but unless you are selling direct B2C, you need to know who you need to sell to and how to sell to them to get your product to the end user.

---

10   Steve Blank, The Startup Owner's Manual: The Step-by-Step Guide for Building a Great Company (Hoboken, New Jersey: John Wiley & Sons, Inc., 2020): 291–355.

- Hire a sales closer: Unless one of the founders is an experienced and successful salesperson, you want to enlist someone who is, but it's important to note that the founder belongs front and center at the selling meetings.

- Align your executives: Your product development and customer development team need to be operating from the same playbook and clearly understand the goals of the company and the plan to obtain those goals.

- Formalize your advisory board: By this juncture, you have had informal advice from a variety of knowledgeable individuals. Now is the time to begin to formalize them as a group. Areas to consider include technical, marketing, business, customers, and industry.

Now It's time to get out of the building again—this time to sell! Set up meetings with your earlyvangelists, and provide them the opportunity to commit to buying your product. The information you discover from this step in the process will help you examine the scalability and repeatability of your hypotheses. Once you've validated your ideas about your customers (you have confirmed people will buy your product), you're ready to bring in more customers and build your business through the *customer creation* phase.

Customer Creation

In the customer creation phase, the main goal is to build demand and awareness for the solution by activating sales channels. Through the customer discovery process, you have acquired significant information regarding your customers—who are they, where are they, how they learn about your product, and where and how they buy it. You also know how your product impacts their life. Equipped with all your customer knowledge, your customer discovery team creates discrete steps to gradually build your business through effective sales channels. It's important to note that there is no branding/marketing/sales team at this stage—this is an iterative process to be thoughtfully and gradually built upon.

Final Checklist

You've decided on an idea to pursue, laid it all out in your Business Model Canvas, and gathered data from your customer discovery process. Now it's time for your final value check, risk check, and gut check before devoting significant time or money to the proposed business.

THE FINAL VALUE CHECK

Based on all the information you've gathered, you'll be able to clearly state the specific problem to be solved by the product or service you plan to offer. You'll know who will benefit from your product or service and how to reach them. You'll know what they think is a fair price. According to the IDEATE authors, the final value check question is this: "Is the idea good for customers, the entrepreneur (me), and stakeholders?"

THE FINAL RISK CHECK

Invention risk is the risk that the idea for a new product can't actually be created or won't actually work. *Execution risk* is the risk of not being able to create and sell a product or service due to logistical problems or lack of resources. *Market risk* is the risk that enough customers won't spend money to buy the product or service for the venture to be profitable. All three risk areas must be considered. If the proposed business idea is too risky, you may need to modify your idea or come up with a new idea. Any new or modified ideas must go through the same testing process you used to evaluate your original idea.

THE FINAL GUT CHECK AND NEXT STEPS

Once you've considered the risks using logic and data, it's time for a less scientific approach. What does your gut say? Many entrepreneurs are famous for their hunches or gut instincts, also called intuition. *Intuition* is an understanding of something based on instinctive feeling rather than conscious reasoning. In 2019, *Inc.* magazine quoted Oprah Winfrey on the subject of intuition: "I've trusted the still, small voice of intuition my entire life. And the only time I've made mistakes is when I didn't listen." When you quiet your mind and pay attention to your "body sense" when you think about a specific question or issue, you give yourself access to your subconscious.

Think about the potential business. Do you get an uplifting, excited feeling, or do you feel a sense of dread? Does something tell you to stop or rethink things, or do you feel energized and ready to move ahead?

Now it's time to determine to pivot or persevere.

Points to Remember

- ➡ The goal of customer discovery is to test a founder's hypotheses and assumptions about their market and customers in order to prove which ones are based in fact.

- ➡ It's critical to remember that during the customer discovery process, the goal is *not* to sell anyone anything; the goal is to garner information that helps you understand your customers' actual needs and how they might be solved.

➡ It's critical through this process that you are open to disinterest in and lack of need for your product. This is information that you will use to reexamine who you thought your customers were *and* the possibility that customers may not exist for your product—at which point, based on those results, it's time to determine whether you should pivot or persevere.

➡ In the customer creation phase, the main goal is to build demand and awareness for the solution by activating sales channels.

Recommended Resources:

➡ *The Mom Test*, by Rob Fitzpatrick

➡ *The Four Steps to the Epiphany: Successful Strategies for Products That Win*, by Steve Blank

➡ *The Startup Owner's Manual: The Step-by-Step Guide for Building a Great Company*, by Steve Blank and Bob Dorf

➡ Steve Blank videos on customer discovery:

- Customer Discovery Preplanning Part 1 Video: https://www.youtube.com/watch?v=0CDDRxF7RlA

- Customer Discovery Preplanning Part 2 Video: https://www.youtube.com/watch?v=YEqyQ9M4hXk

- Customer Discovery Preplanning Part 3 Video: https://www.youtube.com/watch?v=sRBPdbbyz8s

➡ Steve Blank videos on interviews:

    ◻ Interviews Pt. 1 Video:
      https://www.youtube.com/watch?v=pxI7QVdFWok

    ◻ Interviews Pt. 2 Video:
      https://www.youtube.com/watch?v=RSYycOwGhaM

    ◻ Asking the Right Questions Video:
      https://www.youtube.com/watch?v=_49ZSNGH9bM

CHAPTER 5

KNOWING WHEN TO PIVOT AND WHEN TO PERSEVERE

I had a product that we pivoted three times before we, unfortunately, decided to no longer pursue it. That product may have failed, but that experience led me to success. I kept following the path that I wanted and utilizing the valuable skills I acquired through those three pivots. I embraced the changes as they came, and six months later, my cofounders and I launched what has become my passion project: Virtual United.

Benny Pekala

Benny Pekala started his first company in his junior year in college, called Birdwell Solutions (customized software, websites, apps, and social media). It's one of the two companies that are still active that he cofounded. Virtual United is the other company (tools built for passionate virtual event coordinators who want to let their attendees enjoy a free-form networking experience just like they would in real life).

Founding a company in college worked well for me. Entrepreneurship isn't for everyone, but I was blessed to be in a supportive environment at University of Wisconsin–Madison. Being a business owner made it harder for me to keep up with my classes, but it also let me learn a lot of new things that I would not have gotten from my college classes. It was an incredible experience, and my first tips for college entrepreneurs are the following:

- Be bold and make the leap.
- Surround yourself with good people who are smarter than you.

My areas of expertise are software development, business development, and operations. Through those experiences, one of the key steps I learned is to build what you think will satisfy your customers. It's usually not the coolest, most complicated product you can dream up, but it's an important first step.

My step two, which comes from my experience building four or five different products with companies that believe in just "seeing how it goes," is to strongly recommend the utilization of Wix's website tool and Figma for prototyping. These tools will enable you to gather early validations. I also recommend getting sign-ups instead of moving right into building your product. It can take months to build your minimum viable product (MVP). I worked on a product whose MVP took six months to build. It was difficult, but we were able to get sign-ups, paying customers, and funding before performing any software development.

"A minimum viable product (MVP) is an early version of a product that is designed to ensure that product vision and strategy are aligned with market needs.

- *Minimum*: the smallest number of capabilities, features, and packaging that ...
- *Viable*: deliver enough value that customers are willing to spend money (or another currency such as personal information) ...
- *Product*: on something they can use today ... not just invest in a future concept, promise, or offer. "[11]

My step three is agile software development, which is a system where you release every two weeks, and you focus on building new features and adaptations through cross-platform development. And lastly, if you are someone who doesn't want to talk to users, you still must do it. You must be in the room with your users because hearing what people think about the product that you built will change the way you look at it and help answer whether you should persevere or pivot.

If you want to become an entrepreneur, build a supportive community, reach out to experienced entrepreneurs—you'll be surprised how many are willing to spend time with you—and read lots of information on how to build a business. *The Lean Startup* was the business bible for me.

---

11   "How to Define Your Minimum Viable Product (MVP)," SparkPost, accessed January 2022, https://www.sparkpost.com/academy/product-managers/how-to-define-mvp-for-growth/.

The Lean Startup Model

Eric Ries, author of *The Lean Startup*, knows all about the importance of a business's decision to pivot or persevere. In *The Lean Startup*, Ries tells entrepreneurs that a great product and hard work in and of themselves will not lead to a successful and sustainable business; rather, it is the boring, mundane details and small individual choices that make or break a start-up. Despite his first company's initial promise of success, he and his cofounder were not yet equipped to develop a process to utilize their product insights to inform them if, when, and how to pivot or persevere. They were innovative, hardworking, and on the cusp of something great, but nevertheless the business failed.

In 2004, Ries and his cofounders launched another business, IMVU (an avatar-based social network). This time, Ries had Steve Blank, creator of the theoretical customer development framework we discussed in chapter 4, as an investor and advisor, and IMVU incorporated Blank's concept of elevating business and marketing functions and engineering and product development to the same level. Ries and his team also chose to buck the traditional business standards that guide start-ups:

> *"At this point in our careers, my cofounders and I are determined to make new mistakes. We do everything wrong: instead of spending years perfecting our technology, we build a minimum viable product, and an early product that is terrible, full of bugs, and crash-your-computer-yes-really stability problems. Then we ship it to our customers way before it's ready. And we charge money for it. After securing initial customers, we change the product constantly—much too fast by traditional*

standards—shipping new versions of our product dozens of times every single day."[12]

After years of experience, study, and the worldwide success of IMVU, Ries formalized his Lean Startup method based on five principles:

1. Entrepreneurs are everywhere.

2. Entrepreneurship is management.

3. Validated learning.

4. Build—measure—learn.

5. Innovation accounting.

In this chapter, I want to focus on Ries's methodology for when to pivot or persevere, so I won't delve into the details of the five principles above. I will, however, encourage you to read, absorb, and then apply his Lean Startup methodology to your next entrepreneurial venture.

Determining When to Pivot and When to Persevere

The Lean Startup model views the products that start-ups build as experiments; the outcome of those experiments is the learning of how to build a sustainable business. At its core is the Build—Measure—Learn feedback loop, and the key to this feedback loop is to minimize the total time through it.

Build: Once your value hypothesis and growth hypothesis have been determined, the goal is to quickly enter the Build phase with a

---

12 Eric Ries, The Lean Startup: How Today's Entrepreneurs Use Continuous Innovation to Create Radically Successful Businesses (New York City: Crown Business 2011): 4.

minimum viable product (MVP) that you can get in front of customers and assess their response to it.

Measure: In this phase, you are measuring your value hypothesis—Does anyone even want this product?—and your growth hypothesis—Is it scalable?

Learn: Utilizing the data from your Measure phase, it's time to set up what Ries refers to as *learning milestones*, creating actionable metrics that enable you to assess the progress of your product, strategy, and growth accurately and objectively.

The loop complete, it's truth time: Should you pivot or persevere? Quickly determining that even one of your hypotheses is false allows a start-up to pivot swiftly and efficiently, saving both time and money. If your hypotheses prove to be correct, you can confidently persevere on the same course, creating and testing new hypotheses until … one of those hypotheses proves to be false, and it's truth time all over again.

When my company failed, I started another company, and what it did then and what it does now are completely different. The only thing that hasn't changed is the customer base we sell to. We initially sold products that were the same as the company's that failed, only now I bought from competitors and put my brand name on them and then sold them. That pivot kept the business on life support for a while, until I had enough information to make the next pivot. The second pivot was becoming a manufacturer's representative for various products sold to those same dealers, creating a private brand of products manufactured to our specs first in Canada, then in China, and finally in India. Those pivots helped the company grow to a certain point. To scale the business, we needed different products. We found stretch-wrap machines that proved to be highly desired by our current customer base. The business continues to succeed because we frequently monitor the evolving needs of our customers and adapt to fit those needs. We certainly did pivot—many times.

Here is what Eric Ries says about pivots: "Pivot: a structured course correction designed to test a new fundamental hypothesis about the product, strategy, and engine of growth."[13]

Ries contends that pivots are the best measurement of a start-up's runway (how many months a business can continue operating before it runs out of money) rather than the standard measurement of a start-up's runway (cash in the bank divided by monthly spend rate). How many pivots can a business get to before they run out of money—the leaner and faster a start-up can continually get through the Build—Measure—Learn feedback loop, the more pivots they can make in a shorter period of time and the better their chances of success.

This is not to suggest that pivoting is easy. Pivots require an objective and open mindset, a purposeful and validated approach, and a bit of courage. After all, the need to pivot means that something along the way failed, and that can be a challenge to accept for some entrepreneurs. But if you are not failing, you are also not learning or innovating. If you persevere when you should pivot, your business will not be able to maintain long-term sustainability. If you pivot for the sake of change rather than because of measurable and validated data that leads you to a pivot, you will waste precious time, money, and morale that will pull your company down.

The leaner and faster a start-up can continually get through the Build—Measure—Learn feedback loop, the more pivots they can make in a shorter period of time and the better their chances of success.

---

13 Eric Ries, *The Lean Startup*: 149.

SOMETIMES A PIVOT LEADS TO A PATH OF PERSEVERANCE

I feel like one of the most important things in starting a business is understanding there will be a lot of trials and tribulations, and sometimes you just have to put your head down and persevere.

Whitney and Julie Teska

That's a lesson Whitney Teska has learned since starting his screen printing business, Orchard Street Press, in 2008. Although Whitney and coowner (and wife) Julie Teska have persevered through the business's many ups and downs, including the COVID-19 pandemic, Orchard Street Press was the result of a pivot from his original music business.

"Sometimes you have to persevere through all the tough times, and then when you make it to the good times, it's all worthwhile. It's especially true for us now in the pandemic to hold on to that attitude of pushing through the current downturn. It's a challenge, but looking at the history of ten thousand years of pandemics, what it's taught us is that every pandemic is followed by an economic boom. We're not seeking a massive profit for the next year or two—we're doing what we need to do to stay smart and focused, so that

we are one of the businesses that still exist when we come out on the other side of the pandemic."

—WHITNEY TESKA

As a teenager, I played in bands, and my parents agreed to let me and my friends start booking shows across the entire country. By the time I was sixteen, we'd leave for a month and a half and travel the entire country playing music. In 1996, the internet was still pretty new, but we were able to use it to communicate with people and set gigs up across the entire country on our own and release our own records. Then we decided to start making T-shirts to advertise our band and sell at our shows. We needed T-shirts made, and we realized that it was easier to make them ourselves than it was to pay somebody else to do it—so we taught ourselves to screen print in our garages.

Whitney continued designing and printing T-shirts and other merchandise for his own bands, managing independent bands, booking tours across the United States and Europe, and negotiating record contracts through his high school and college years. By 2008, with ten years of experience in the music industry and the realization that there was a need in the music business that he could fill—screen printed merchandise—he opened Orchard Street Press.

What really helped get the business going was winning the La Macchia New Venture Business Plan Competition at the University of Wisconsin—Milwaukee in early 2008. The $10,000 prize was enough to start the business. From there, Julie and I spent several years barely paying ourselves and reinvesting all the money back into the business. It seemed like every time we turned around, there was something new to buy, but since we hadn't yet established enough credit history, we weren't able to go out and buy brand-new equipment—we always bought used. When we moved out of our basement and into our first building, we spent about $20,000 on used automatic equipment. We didn't buy our first 100 percent completely brand-new press until February 2020.

Today, Orchard Street Press is a thriving business in the Milwaukee, Wisconsin, area. In 2011, Whitney and Julie expanded their product offerings with the launching of their own product line that includes clothing and accessories for men, women, children, and babies that is sold in various boutiques and shops around Wisconsin and the Midwest.

Whether you decide to quickly pivot multiple times as Benny did with one of his first products or engage in multiple interests as Whitney did before choosing which path to follow and persevere, the key is to make those decisions intentionally (Ries recommends a regularly scheduled pivot-or-persevere meeting) via a scientific methodology while channeling the human elements of vision, intuition, and judgment.

Points to Remember

➡ It's important to purposely and continually assess whether your business should pivot or persevere.

➡ The decision to pivot or persevere must be founded in objective and proven data.

➡ Create products that fill a customer need and that customers will buy—creating something shiny and new that no one will buy will not succeed.

➡ The first iteration of your product should be an MVP that is tested on a finite group of early adopters.

Recommended Resources

➡ *The Lean Startup*, by Eric Ries

➡ *The Student Startup Guide*, by Dave Gee

CHAPTER 6

CREATING AND REFINING YOUR BUSINESS PLAN

During her first two years of high school, Loren Nelson had a part-time job coaching and instructing youth tennis for eight dollars an hour. At sixteen, she gave her first private tennis lesson and charged thirty dollars an hour. That was a turning point for Loren and the moment she decided never to settle for less than she was worth, and so began her journey of entrepreneurship. Loren went on to found and run two businesses while completing her undergraduate studies as a marketing major at the University of Wisconsin—Milwaukee (UWM). Here's how she made that happen.

In high school, I made money as a fitness instructor, personal trainer, and tennis instructor. I hosted workout groups at my home and offered personal training sessions. I got professionally certified as a tennis coach and offered private tennis lessons for eighty to ninety dollars per hour. In college, I decided I wanted to start a facial products company. My parents were very supportive. My mother was just starting to ramp up her own business. My dad offered to help fund my start-up, and he encouraged me to go for it.

Loren Nelson

I didn't really have mentors at the beginning. I watched a lot of YouTube videos and listened to podcasts to learn about business in general. People in the Lubar Entrepreneurship Center were helpful when I was working on my Business Model Canvas and business plan, and the Student Startup Challenge pop-up sessions were good. I also attended leadership dinners sponsored by the multicultural center that had interesting keynote speakers. Another support system was a great group of friends. When we'd hang out, we'd spark ideas and kind of uplift each other. So, in a way, they were mentors, too.

I entered several student business competitions, and the work I did on my business plan really paid off, winning me $18,000 total in prize money from one state-level competition and four school-related competitions. I took some of the same skills I'd learned coaching and teaching tennis— pitching myself to parents to coach their kids—and I figured out how to position my messaging to effectively sell my business and my products.

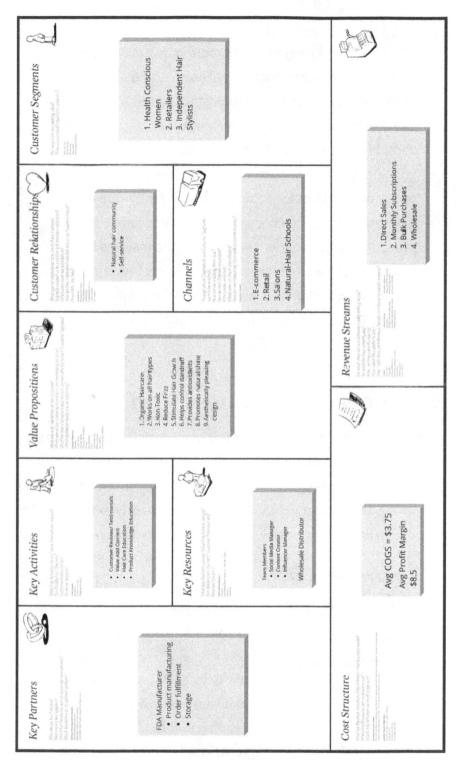

Lёvor Business Model Canvas

I started Lëvor during my sophomore year in college, initially as a facial products company. Then I shifted to custom-made wigs and then switched over to organic hair care. My latest venture, Dream Vallie Success Journal (dreamvallie. com) launched in 2020, and I'm building up my YouTube and social media presence. The success journal is based on my own system for setting goals, organizing tasks, and motivating myself to succeed. A lot of that comes from my years of athletic experience and having to manage my time to balance school, tennis training, and a part-time job. With Lëvor, I'm working on slowly scaling internationally and making the shift to an all-wholesale business.

Creating Your Business Plan

The business plan outlines the major characteristics of a company, including its planned product or service, industry, potential or existing market, organizational structure, assets and resources, operations, marketing and sales strategies, and projected financial outcomes. An entrepreneur needs a business plan for a variety of reasons—the primary reason being to obtain funding. Banks and potential investors will review the business plan as part of their decision-making process. The SBA website (https://www.sba.gov/business-guide/plan-your-business/write-your-business-plan#section-header-2) describes how to write a business plan and supplies

An entrepreneur needs a business plan for a variety of reasons—the primary reason being to obtain funding.

some sample plans. However, their suggested formats for business plans are not examples that I endorse—the writers of these sample plans would not pass the entrepreneurship course that I teach at UWM! See the appendices to this book for an outline entitled "How to Write a Business Plan for a New Venture."

College students can enter business plan contests, and winners often receive seed money to help with starting a new enterprise. For example, students at the University of Wisconsin–Milwaukee can enter several annual business plan competitions, including the Wisconsin Governor's Business Plan Contest (winners share $100,000), the UWM Schoenfeld Entrepreneurial Awards Competition ($5,000–$15,000 per each winner), the UWM I a Macchia New Venture Business Plan Competition ($10,000, $5,000, and $2,500 prizes). Contests awarding similar prize money are held at schools all over the country. Others are sponsored by private foundations and community organizations.

The following sections describe the essential components of the business plan.

COVER LETTER

Typical cover letters are one page and include the following:

- An introduction of yourself, your business, and the reasons you are submitting your business plan to this individual or group (mention any referrals or prior contacts)

- The purpose/fundamental goal of your company

- The major aspects of your planned enterprise

- The current status of the company

- A thank-you to the reader for their consideration and your next step

COVER, TITLE PAGE, AND TABLE OF CONTENTS

The cover and title page includes the following:

- Company name (and logo if you have created one)

- Your name and contact information

- The date the plan was produced

The table of contents should list all the major section headings (including appendices) with their corresponding page numbers.

EXECUTIVE SUMMARY

While an elevator pitch is a sixty-second verbal summary of your business used to entice the listener to ask for a time to learn more, the executive summary is a one- to two-page narrative that provides a high-level overview of the business and assumes the reader has some level of knowledge of or interest in your business. It should address the problem, the product or service that solves the problem, the market, your competitive advantage, the current status of the business, a brief financial summary, brief bios of the owner and key members of the business team, and the "ask" (if investment is being requested).

THE COMPANY

This section describes the company and its product or service in more detail, describing the problem that your product/service is designed to solve, how the product/service will benefit customers, and its competitive advantage.

THE MARKET

This section describes your target market in terms of scope and scale. You'll identify who your potential customers are (including supporting data and demographic information), determine the dollar value if the product/service is sold to every applicable customer, and verify that the market is large enough to be worth the effort and risk. Depending on the stage of your business, you may also want to include a growth plan. Be sure to include the dollar value of the specific market you are addressing. What would that dollar value be if you sold products or services to obtain 100 percent of that market? This will tell you whether the total market that you are addressing is worth the effort.

LEGAL AND ORGANIZATIONAL STRUCTURE

In this section you describe the company's legal and tax status (e.g., partnership, LLC, corporation, etc.); where the business is registered; and any licenses, certifications, patents, or trademarks that apply. You'll also need to list a physical business address, website (if applicable), and members of a board of directors (if applicable) and key personnel, including their roles and a brief description of their background and qualifications. Be careful to mention who the decision maker(s) is. Some investors will not consider investing in a start-up unless one person has voting control in the business (51 percent ownership). This is not a hard-and-fast rule, but it is the rule for some investors. Simple partnerships and sole proprietorships, in my opinion, are not feasible options. The legal form of an organization should shield the owners from personal liability if the business fails or incurs significant legal liability.

FINANCIAL SUMMARY

This is a three-page document showing projected costs, sales, and profits, combined with another document showing the statement of financial assumptions. Supporting documentation is provided as an appendix, and interactive versions of all these forms can be found on my website (www.jameshhunter.com). Investors frequently are accounting and financially oriented individuals who look for financial information in standard financial forms—income statement, balance sheet, and statement of cash flow. Typically, for an existing business, two years' prior data are provided. For start-ups, supporting details are provided by month for the first year and by year for the following two years.

FUNDING REQUEST

This is where you make your request for funds (the "ask"), stating how much money is needed and how it will be used. When seeking investors, this section will describe what is being offered in exchange for their support (e.g., seat on the board, share of the business, interest rate and payment terms if a loan investment, percentage return on their investment) and an exit plan should they decide to withdraw from the business.

APPENDICES

The appendices provide detailed information in support of the sales and revenue projections made in the plan. In addition to detailed financial data, they may include product or service photos (and/or illustrations or specifications), facility layouts or floor plans, copies of relevant contracts, results of customer discovery / market research, price lists, testimonials, résumés of key personnel, and promotional/advertising material. While not all advisors agree, in my experience it seems that adding color to the business plan cover, having color photos interspersed in the plan, and using color charts can add interest and further engage the reader of the plan.

Now that you know what type of information is needed in your business, let's move on to selling your products and services, as well as the business plan itself!

Points to Remember

➡ A business model is the rationale and framework for how a business will make a profit.

➡ The business plan is a written description of the business concept and the resources and steps needed to launch the business and make it successful.

➡ Writing and presenting a clear, complete business plan is an essential part of obtaining funding for a start-up or expansion and for winning competitions.

➡ Business plans are often presented in person as part of business competitions and when meeting with potential investors.

Recommended Resources

Interactive financial report templates are available at www.jamesh-hunter.com, including financial statement assumptions, income statements, balance sheets, and statements of financial cash flow.

You can also find copies of these templates in the appendices of this book, in addition to other resources in the appendices such as how to write a business plan, Bygrave and Zacharakis's Opportunity Checklist, and the judges' evaluation form for the New Venture Ideation Award. And, while you can find sample business plans from the SBA online (https://www.sba.gov/business-guide/plan-your-business/write-your-business-plan#section-header-2), their samples wouldn't get very good grades in the business plan class taught at UWM! Compare them to an outstanding example of a business plan done by UW–M students on my website, www.jameshhunter.com.

CHAPTER 7

MAKING IT REAL—SALES

Isaac Hetzroni grew up in an entrepreneurial environment. Both his grandfathers and his father were lifelong entrepreneurs, and they instilled that mindset in him at a young age.

Ever since I was a little kid, I was told, "We're not going to give you money. We'll give you the lemons, and you can go make a lemonade stand." At five years old, I was working at my grandfather's dancewear production facility in Toronto making swatches. Earning two dollars a day at the age of five gave me a good understanding of the work-money relationship. If I worked a whole day, it was going to turn into this amount of money, and then this amount of money could go and turn into little products. My earnings netted me a collection of small vending machine toys, and when I grew tired of the toys, I sold them.

When I was in middle school, I bought a pair of Beats by Dre and realized that the supplier was selling them refurbished. I did some investigating and found that the headphones could be purchased from China for three dollars and that I could sell them for twenty dollars. Everyone at school wanted them, and I made $4,000 that year. I also bought my first existing business while in middle school. A fellow student was selling hats, and I bought his company for $400, acquiring his Facebook page and all of his clients. I started growing my empire—until I was sent to the principal's office too many times for putting too many flyers all over school.

Isaac Hetzroni and team

Despite his run-in with the principal, his parents encouraged his entrepreneurial efforts, and Isaac clearly had a knack for seeing what his market wanted and how to sell it to them.

In high school, I started a Junior Achievement company at my school. I saw an opportunity within the health-snack standards in which students weren't allowed to go and sell unhealthy foods anymore. I created a fundraising solution that then turned into a branding and marketing solution for health food companies. We had clients like Clif Bar and Zico, who not only had a tough time getting market data on whether a customer liked the new flavors, but it was also difficult for them to get their samples in front of customers without paying all this money for activations.

To solve the problem, the companies would send us pallets full of free samples, and we would package them into sample bags and sell the bags at a discount to schools and health food stores. We collected tons of user feedback and data on how people were enjoying the snacks. That was a cool business, and in a couple of months we made around $8,000 profit, breaking the record for highest profit for a Junior Achievement company.

In his freshman year at the University of Florida, Isaac found a product that gained the attention of his fellow students: a small fan that plugs into your cell phone. He brought the "plug-in fan" to a party attended by his classmates, and it was an instant hit. Isaac's sales pitch was this: "They're five bucks, and I'm Isaac, the fan guy. Give me your phone number and Snapchat, and we can meet up when I have more fans." Isaac collected fifteen preorders that day, so he ordered a hundred online. Within the first week, they were all sold. He was quite excited about this business. It gave him the opportunity to meet girls and make money. Life couldn't be better! Next, he ordered a thousand with the school's logo on it, which sold within a couple of weeks. Soon his friends at other schools wanted to start selling them, and the business continued to grow.

Officials from Isaac's hometown contacted him and asked if he could put the city name on the fans. He agreed to have that done and reduced the price to four dollars each. Isaac made so much money selling them in bulk as a promo item and selling in bulk was so much easier that he decided that it was better selling thousands to one customer rather than one at a time to thousands of customers. He changed the business model to selling a one-hundred-piece minimum. He learned that the promotion business is a $25 billion industry, and he didn't think the industry had many interesting products. Isaac continued to pursue the bulk promotion business and made $45,000 the first year. He has now graduated, and his enterprise Imprint Genius is a $2 million per year business.

Through his eagerness to make money and have fun doing it, along with his ability to identify products that will sell and how to sell them, Isaac was willing to put himself out there and take risks to make his businesses a reality.

Making It Real Through Sales

I understand that the art of selling doesn't come easily to everyone—in fact, I'm one of those people. I don't particularly like sales, but when you're in business for yourself, especially in the beginning when you *are* the business, being a salesperson is a necessity. Through that necessity, I have listened, read, and learned what successful selling practices look like. The resource I refer to most in this area is Neil Rackham's *SPIN Selling*.

> *When you're in business for yourself, especially in the beginning when you are the business, being a salesperson is a necessity.*

Through their research, Rackham and his team at Huthwaite began to question the long-held belief that successful salespeople are successful because they are able to close by implementing a variety of closing techniques. While he found this to be true for the small-scale sales—low-cost items sold in one sales call—it did not appear to translate to large-scale sales. In fact, assertive closing techniques in large-scale sales seemed to negatively impact the sale.

A primary reason for this finding is the psychological impact of pressure. As Rackham explains, "If I'm asking you to make a very small decision, then—if I pressure you—it's easier for you to say yes than have an argument. Consequently, with a small decision, the effect of pressure is positive. But this isn't so with large decisions. The bigger the decision, the more negatively people generally react to pressure."[14]

Rackham realized that large-scale selling required more complexity and sophistication to help the buyer understand the value of the purchase for their needs and often required a longer selling strategy. It is this revelation that prompted the creation of the SPIN model. SPIN selling is based on a distinctive sequence of positive questions utilized during the investigating stage of a sales call.

THE FOUR STAGES OF A SALES CALL

1. Preliminaries: Critical initial impressions before the selling begins.

2. Investigating: Uncovering needs and gaining a better understanding of your customer.

3. Demonstrating capability: Demonstrating why your product or service provides a valuable solution for your customer.

---

14   Neil Rackham, SPIN Selling: The Best-Validated Sales Method Available Today. Developed from Research Studies of 35,000 Sales Calls. Used by the Top Sales Forces across the World (United States of America: McGraw-Hill, 1988): 30.

4. Obtaining commitment: At the end of the call, the intent is to have some form of commitment from the customer: sale, product demonstration, access to a higher-level decision maker.

Here is how Racham's SPIN selling acronym plays out:

Situation questions: These are questions asked at the start of the sales call to help you understand the buyer's current situation. "How long have you had your present equipment?" "What are your current processes?"

Problem questions: This next phase of questioning occurs once sufficient information has been gathered on the buyer's situation. These questions help highlight the different problems your product solves for this buyer. "Is this operation difficult to perform?" "Are you worried about the quality you get from your machine?"

Implication questions: In smaller sales, sellers are often successful simply by asking situational and problem questions. Not so in large-scale sales, which require more complex and sophisticated questions to help your customer understand their problem's urgency and that the investment in your product or service is worthwhile. "How will this problem affect your future profitability?" "What does this turnover mean in terms of training costs?"

Need-payoff questions: When done successfully, need-payoff questions get your customer to tell *you* the benefits that your solution would provide them. "Would it be useful to speed this operation by 10 percent?" "Would a comprehensive product management tool increase stakeholder buy-in?"

Rackham emphasizes that although the bulk of each section of questions is asked in the SPIN order, it is not a rigid sequence. A seasoned salesperson will know when to move to the next question in the sequence and/or return to a previous one.

Sales is a process that takes practice and an understanding of the nuances of your product or services and your customers. Take the time to research sales techniques to find the ones that can be adapted to work for you, and like Rackham, don't be afraid to challenge "tried and true" beliefs.

Entrepreneurs Don't Just Sell Product

Going into business isn't just about selling your products or services to your potential customers. An entrepreneur must also sell their vision, purpose, and the sustainability of their business to appropriate stake-holders. We outlined the components of a business plan in chapter 6. Now it's time to make that business plan real by getting it in front of people who you need buy-in from.

EVALUATING YOUR PLAN

You've created your business plan—now it's time to evaluate it. Alan Katz, owner and president of Katz Consulting, LLC, and his team have reviewed hundreds of business plans written by students in my entrepreneurship class. They developed criteria for evaluating the plans using a one-to-seven rating scale. They look for clear communication and appropriate and appealing use of graphics, charts, and tables. You can use their criteria to take a hard look at your plan and see where you might need to do some updating or revising to clarify and strengthen it so that you can confidently sell it. You can find the complete evaluation document at www.jameshhunter.com as well as in this book's appendices.

For each section of the plan, Alan and his associate ask these questions:

- Is this area covered in adequate detail?

- Does the plan show a clear understanding of the elements that should be addressed?

- Are the assumptions realistic and reasonable?

- Are the risks identified, and is the ability to manage those risks addressed?

Once you've gotten the plan hammered out and done your self-evaluation, it's a good idea to ask your advisors and mentors to review the plan and provide feedback before you finalize it. And remember the importance of proofreading. If you don't have the most critical eye, ask a friend or colleague with proofreading skills to do a read-through to check for errors in language, grammar, spelling, punctuation, math, and formatting. Errors distract readers and reduce your credibility, and you want your plan to shine!

PREPARING FOR AN IN-PERSON PRESENTATION

Once your business plan is ready, it's time to present it to your prospects. There are two main components to in-person presentations—the elevator pitch and your pitch deck. Once you have these prepared, it's important to practice your presentation until you feel comfortable with it. You want to communicate your passion for the business, your expertise, and your professionalism. Wearing appropriate business attire and being well groomed are essential.

Once you begin speaking, you want to make a sincere and meaningful connection with your audience. When you practice, focus on speaking clearly and with enthusiasm. Make eye contact and smile as you speak. Try to anticipate questions you may be asked, and be prepared to give honest answers. Honesty is very important. On the big day, if you don't have the answer to a specific question, simply say so. If you need to do more research about something, you can promise to follow up with an answer within a short period of time.

The Elevator Pitch

The elevator pitch is a brief presentation (no more than sixty seconds or two hundred words) that provides a dynamic explanation of your business. It includes a "hook" to lure readers or listeners in and make them want to learn more. The pitch is used to attract customers or investors and sell them on the need for your product or service.[15]

Slide Presentation: The Pitch Deck

When presenting your business plan in person, you'll generally be given about fifteen minutes to address your audience, followed by a period for questions. You'll need to put together a slide presentation that highlights key aspects of your business plan in a clear and visually appealing way. Slides usually cover these topics:

- Introduction to you and the company

- Problem facing the market

- Solution your company offers and why the solution is valid

- Product/service—a bit more detail

- Market description and size

- Business model

- Competition

---

15   Northeastern University's School of Business offers tips for crafting an effective
      pitch along with examples. Visit https://onlinebusiness.northeastern.edu/
      master-of-business-administration-mba/knowledge/elevator-pitch-guide/pitch-examples/.

- Founder and management team

- Financial highlights

- The "ask" (investment opportunity)

- Closing—thanking the audience and asking for questions

If you don't have the opportunity to present your pitch deck in person, I recommend that you send it digitally to your stakeholders along with your business plan. However, presenting in person is so important that you should try to hold out for an in-person presentation if you can.

EVALUATING AND REFINING YOUR BUSINESS PLAN

Once you've presented your business plan a few times, make any necessary revisions based on the questions and responses that you're hearing to make sure that you are communicating the right message to potential investors and other audiences.

Points to Remember

- ➡ The elevator pitch is a brief presentation that provides an explanation of the business and a "hook" to lure readers or listeners in and make them want to learn more.

- ➡ The pitch deck is a set of slides that highlight key aspects of the business plan in a clear and visually appealing way.

- ➡ It's essential to practice an in-person presentation of your business plan ahead of time until you feel comfortable and can easily communicate your enthusiasm and expertise.

- ➡ Business plans are dynamic and will likely need to be evaluated, revised, and updated as the business evolves.

Recommended Resources:

➡ Elevator pitch guide: https://onlinebusiness.northeastern. edu/master-of-business-administration-mba/knowledge/ elevator-pitch-guide/pitch-examples/

➡ *SPIN Selling*, by Neil Rackham

CHAPTER 8

UNDERSTANDING LEGAL AND TAX ISSUES

Seeking legal and tax advice is not what excites most new entrepreneurs. It can be confusing and overwhelming, not to mention expensive, but assuring that your business meets its legal requirements from the outset is essential. Having to fix legal issues down the road can cost you your business. Melissa Zabkowicz—an associate with Reinhart Boerner Van Deuren s.c.; a member of the data privacy and cybersecurity team; and an advisor in mergers and acquisitions, commercial transactions, securities compliance, entity formation, and general corporate governance—advises students at the University of Wisconsin–Milwaukee (UWM) in the areas of legal forms of organization and corporate legal matters. I met with Melissa to learn what she believes are the critical legal and tax steps new entrepreneurs must take.

First Things First

1. Solidify Your Company Name and Logo

Your company's name and logo are how your customers will find you, so you want to get it right the first time around. Check with your state's registered businesses database to make sure the name you want is not already taken. It's important that you also run a trademark search with the US Patent and Trademark Office to ensure that your idea for a name is not infringing on another company. Businesses who don't do their homework risk having to make a name change in the future, which has the potential to significantly disrupt the company's ability to do business.

One of my companies selected a name that was not taken in the state of Wisconsin (Global Handling, Inc.), but it was close enough to other companies' names (Global Industrial, Global Industrial Equipment, and Global Equipment) as to cause confusion.

Global Handling, Inc., was created to sell material-handling equipment to end users. The name was created, and then a company catalog with the thousands of products that we sold was created with "Global Handling" imprinted on it. We would send the catalog out to hundreds of people who would then either call or mail in their orders; we would fill the order and bill them for the products, and they would mail us a check.

One day we received a check in the mail, and we didn't know what it was for because we didn't have an order associated with it. That's when we noticed that the check was made out to Global Industrial rather than Global Handling. We looked up Global Industrial, a major catalog company in New York, and realized a mistake had been made. We attached a note to the check and sent it to Global Industrial, thinking that that would be the end of it.

Well, we received the piece of mail that every business dreads—the one with an attorney's return address, which is often either an invoice or a lawsuit. Global Industrial was threatening to sue us because we had a name that was infringing on its name. The name test is whether the name would be confusing to people who are somehow involved in the business, and our name was obviously confusing to customers. We didn't fight it. We agreed that we would change our name, and we told them that. Global Industrial ended its threat to sue, and we went through the painful process of changing our name to Optimal Handling Solutions.

Of course, our existing customers had never heard of Optimal Handling Solutions, so when we sent out our new catalogs, they thought it was a brand-new company that they didn't know anything about. We did our best to explain that it was just a name change, but many of our customers just didn't get it, and as a result our sales dropped 30 percent. We were tasked with changing our website, our catalogs, our stationary, our invoices, and any promotional materials to the new name and then promoting the product under the new name to grow our customer base back. It was a costly mistake that took us two years to build back up.

Our previous name had built up equity that was lost because we infringed on a nationally registered name. Any new company should not make this same mistake. Check nationally when you create your company's name.

2. Decide Who You Are Going into Business With

One of the most important decisions an entrepreneur can make is who to go into business with. Whether you have a partner(s) or investor(s), it's important to remember that these are individuals who are giving money and/or time to your business, and they care about what happens to their investment. An investor can be a family member, a friend, or a third-party investor such as a private equity or venture capital company. Regardless of whether it's your mom, best friend, or an outside investor, a governance document must be developed to establish how much money they invested and the detail of what that money gets them.

Splitting equity among cofounders can be a difficult decision, but it is a very important one. Often cofounders do not spend adequate time sorting out the equity split. There are entrepreneurs who claim that an equal 25 percent equity split among four founders of a new venture will lead to disaster. Some investors who evaluate business plans for the entrepreneurship class at the University of Wisconsin–Milwaukee say that they will not invest in a small company that does not have one 51+ percent owner. These investors say that they do not want to have to deal with more than one founder and that several founders involved in major decisions make the decision process long and complicated.

The Babson College Research Translation Showcase in 2017 offered the summary "How to Split Equity among Cofounders to Achieve Satisfaction," authored by Eva Weissenböck of the Technical University of Munich, Germany. In this summary, several suggestions were made on how to arrive at the best equity split. The final conclusion in this summary was that "agreeing on moderate levels of equity inequality might lead to cofounders being most satisfied with their teams."

This document is typically in the form of an operating agreement for an LLC or a shareholder agreement for the LLC or for the corporation, and it governs exactly how investors are treated, what they receive, and what their rights are for controlling the company. This document is vital to assure that everyone understands what's happening. For example, investors who aren't involved in the business should not have significant control over the business—the owner/founder should retain that control. The operating agreement or shareholder agreement establishes the voting rights for each investor; for example, they may have a vote in dissolving the company or buying another company, but they don't have any rights in the control of daily operations. What about monies they receive? The governance must make clear that an investment is just that, an investment, which means they are taking a risk, and if things go bad, they won't receive any money back. If the investment is in the form of a loan, that must also be clearly spelled out so that everyone's expectations are on the same page.

A key factor in any business arrangement with more than one person is trust. If you don't trust your partners and investors and they don't trust you, you shouldn't be in business together.

A key factor in any business arrangement with more than one person is trust. If you don't trust your partners and investors and they don't trust you, you shouldn't be in business together.

3. Form a Legal Entity

Now that you know who you're going into business with or whether you are going to be a sole owner, it's time to form a legal entity to protect the owner(s) of the company from personal liability exposure. Let's face it, things can go wrong with the running of a business, and if it does, you want to make sure you (and your partners) are legally protected. A simple (although potentially catastrophic) liability example for a business is when a customer slips and falls on the business's premises. Say a customer falls in a restaurant; they can sue and come after the restaurant's assets for compensation. But if properly set up, the company's legal entity status will prevent them from coming after the restaurant owner's personal assets.

Under no circumstances should anyone open a business without forming a legal entity. The question then becomes, "Which type of business entity should I form?" The entity you choose will determine your tax structure. The most common forms are the following:[16]

- **Sole Proprietorships**: A sole proprietor is someone who owns an unincorporated business by themselves. However, if you are the sole member of a domestic limited liability company (LLC), you are not a sole proprietor if you elect to treat the LLC as a corporation. In the entrepreneurship course that I teach, it is made clear that no new entrepreneur should organize their business as a sole proprietorship or a simple partnership—solely because of the unlimited personal liability inherent in those organizational structures.

- **Partnerships:** A partnership is a relationship between two or more people. Each person contributes money, property, and labor or skill and shares in the profits and losses of the business.

- **Corporations:** In forming a corporation, prospective shareholders exchange money, property, or both for the corporation's capital stock. A corporation generally takes the same

---

16   IRS, "Business Structures," accessed April 2022, https://www.irs.gov/businesses/small-businesses-self-employed/business-structures.

deductions as a sole proprietorship to figure its taxable income. A corporation can also take special deductions. For federal income tax purposes, a C corporation is recognized as a separate taxpaying entity. A corporation conducts business, realizes net income or loss, pays taxes, and distributes profits to shareholders.

- **S Corporations:** S corporations are corporations that elect to pass corporate income, losses, deductions, and credits through to their shareholders for federal tax purposes. Shareholders of S corporations report the flow-through of income and losses on their personal tax returns and are assessed tax at their individual income tax rates. This allows S corporations to avoid double taxation on the corporate income. S corporations are responsible for tax on certain built-in gains and passive income at the entity level

- **Limited Liability Company:** A limited liability company (LLC) is a business structure allowed by state statute. Each state may use different regulations; you should check with your state if you are interested in starting a limited liability company. Owners of an LLC are called members. Most states do not restrict ownership, so members may include individuals, corporations, other LLCs, and foreign entities. There is no maximum number of members. Most states also permit "single-member" LLCs (those having only one owner).

It is in an owner's best interest to consult a tax advisor *and* corporate law attorney when making this determination.

Melissa advises that in recent years the default entity status for a new business—over 70 percent—is an LLC. This legal form of organization can be set up by the entrepreneur online generally for a cost of less than $200. (Some universities such as the University of Wisconsin–Milwaukee will cover the fee for a student to set up an LLC.) The sequence of events is as follows:

I.   Go to your state's department of financial institutions, create an approved name (one that no other entity has in your state), create articles of organization, and pay a fee (in Wisconsin the electronic articles of organization fee is $130, and the name reservation fee is $15). *Before you finalize the name of your business,* check with the US Patent and Trademark Office to be sure that no one else has the name you select or a similar name.

II. Then visit the IRS website for how to apply for an EIN (employer identification number).[17] You can obtain an EIN at no charge. Some websites charge for this service, but you do not need to pay a fee. Once you have the required form filled out with your EIN, make a copy for your file.

III. Next, open a bank account distinct from any personal account. You must not mingle personal finances with your company's finances. If mingled, it makes it unclear what are the company's assets and what are yours.

4.   Create Standard Terms and Conditions for Your Product and/or Services

As consumers, we all dread slogging through a company's or product's terms and conditions, but there's a reason every company should have them for the products and services they sell: it limits the liability of the company. Terms and conditions protect a company

---

17   IRS, "How to Apply for an EIN," accessed April 2022, https://www.irs.gov/businesses/small-businesses-self-employed/how-to-apply-for-an-ein.

from things out of their control. Some examples of what terms and conditions enable companies to do this are the following:

- Withdraw and cancel services

- Disable user accounts

- Manage customer expectations

- Set rules for user behavior

If a customer claims that your services or products harmed them or didn't work properly, the terms and conditions keep them from coming after more than is reasonable.

5. Have Critical Contracts Reviewed by an Attorney

Businesses may require loans, equipment, and resources that require legal contracts. Complicated contracts can be challenging for an attorney to decipher. For someone who is not trained in law, it can be impossible to understand the intricacies of a thirty-page contract. There are some simple contracts that may not need a lawyer's review, but for contracts related to leasing, financing, investing, and the like, it is prudent to have an attorney thoroughly review and explain it to you. The rule of thumb is this: "If the contract seems complicated, have a qualified attorney review it prior to signing."

How contract disputes will be handled should be included in the contract. There are three principal ways to handle such disputes: (1) mediation, the least expensive and most expeditious; (2) arbitration, which is more expensive and more time consuming; and (3) litigation, which is very expensive and very time consuming. Here is some sound advice: "You never want to enter into litigation if it can be avoided." Always review the method for settling disputes when signing a contract, and decide what makes the most sense for you and the business.

A lender will want to see the new business's organization documents. For an LLC the document is called an operating agreement. The best form of operating agreement is prepared by an attorney, and it fits your situation. However, while risky, for one of my start-ups that was really short of cash, I used a "canned" operating agreement obtained from www.legalzoom.com. I got the loan, and soon after that I had an attorney prepare a more suitable operating agreement.

Legal and Tax Professionals

All businesses should have an attorney relationship in some form from the beginning. Legal issues will arise for all businesses from time to time, and it's best to have an established relationship prior to a serious legal challenge. A new start-up can sometimes find a good small business attorney in a small local law firm to help on legal issues at modest hourly rates. Creative arrangements can also be made with a legal advisor who can provide the advice needed at a modest cost.

It is also sometimes possible to obtain legal counsel as a part of the business team. This could involve granting an equity interest. While not a qualified legal advisor, an experienced mentor can help resolve issues that could escalate to a legal issue if not handled immediately and properly and advise when legal counsel should be retained. Entrepreneurs should consider seminars and webinars to educate themselves in legal matters, including how to recognize when an attorney is needed and when the entrepreneur can handle the issue without an attorney.

Entrepreneurs should also enlist the services of an accountant/tax professional early on. While attorneys can advise as to the type of legal entity that best suits your business needs and to some extent your tax entity, it is an accountant who will have the most knowledge regarding what makes the most sense for your business from a taxation perspective and be able to provide expert advice on making sure your financials are in order. Even small start-ups must make sure their financial records are done correctly from the beginning.

Points to Remember

➡ Don't risk having to make a costly name change! Check with your state's registered businesses database to make sure the name you want is not already taken. It's important that you also run a trademark search with the US Patent and Trademark Office to assure that your idea for a name is not infringing on another company.

➡ Choose whom you go into business with wisely, and execute a governance document at the onset to clearly establish roles and details of the agreed-upon equity split.

➡ Under no circumstances should anyone open a business without forming a legal entity. The status you choose determines your personal liability and tax structure.

➡ Seek legal advice before you get started. If you can't afford to hire an attorney, seek out those who may assist you in your family-and-friend circle and research organizations like the SBA or your school who may be able to offer assistance in these areas.

Recommended Resources

➡ IRS, Business Structures: https://www.irs.gov/businesses/ small-businesses-self-employed/business-structures

➡ IRS, How to Apply for an EIN: https://www.irs.gov/businesses/ small-businesses-self-employed/how-to-apply-for-an-ein

➡ "How to Split Equity among Cofounders to Achieve Satisfaction," authored by Eva Weissenböck of the Technical University of Munich, Germany, https://www.babson.edu/media/babson/ assets/bcerc-dc-translations/WeissenbÄck-Research--Translation-2020.pdf

CHAPTER 9

MASTERING THE NUMBERS

"My plan is to wait until after the close of the year to review my financials." That was Bill's response to my question about whether he had been reviewing monthly financial statements during his first year of business. Bill was a good friend of mine and a customer, and this conversation took place at a party he hosted in December to celebrate his success. At that time he had twenty employees, and the business appeared to be thriving. Still, I couldn't help but have concerns about his lack of regular financial review during his start-up year. Here's Bill's story.

Bill was a top sales representative at the forklift dealership that I called on as a sales representative for a forklift attachments manufacturer. He had been with the dealership for ten years, first as a sales representative and then later promoted to sales manager. Everybody loved Bill. He was personable, responsible, attentive, and reliable—all the characteristics of an all-around good guy. Bill had thought about starting his own business, and all he needed was my encouragement to pull the trigger.

In January, Bill had begun his business, reconditioning and selling used forklift trucks. Bill knew the ins and outs of buying used forklifts and how to manage his staff to make minor repairs and paint to prepare the used trucks for sale. The business grew quickly. Bill would buy a used forklift, receive a bank loan to cover a healthy percentage of the purchase price, fix it up, and sell it. There was always money in the bank as Bill financed his purchases and received payment for the reconditioned trucks that he sold.

Fast-forward to my conversation with him at his December celebration. Based on Bill's lack of regular financial review during his first twelve months of starting his business, it appeared that he had been managing his business out of his checkbook. As long as he had cash in his bank account, he felt that things were fine on the financial front. To say that a business's finances cannot be managed via a company's checkbook is a significant understatement. At the very least, those numbers could be misleading, and in Bill's case this was especially true because of his continual loans to support the purchase of another used forklift truck. Such a process could result in a sort of "Ponzi scheme" in which new money was always there to pay off old debts as the business grew. In this scenario, any slowing of growth could result in cash shortages. If profits were high enough, the cash needs could be satisfied out of profits on forklift truck sales. If profits were low, a cash bind could occur. The only way to know the true profits and financial health of any business is to review timely financial statements.

> *A business's finances cannot be managed via a company's checkbook.*

I next spoke with Bill in February after he received his first financial statements. His financials revealed that he had been losing money every month of the start-up year and that he was in dire financial straits. The entire organization came crashing down in April, and Bill had to file for bankruptcy. He lost the business and his self-confidence.

If there is one clear lesson to learn from Bill's painful experience, it's *review your monthly financial statements!* At a minimum, your income statement (also called a profit and loss (P&L) statement), your balance sheet, and your cash flow statement should be reviewed monthly. You can find templates of these in this book's appendices as well as on my website, www.jameshhunter.com.

If Bill had been warned of his financial problems during the previous spring, he would have had time to make corrections that may have saved the business.

Show Me the Numbers

When a business owner seeks funding to start or grow their business, they can speak passionately about their product or their fantastic marketing plan all day long, but the funder, be it a bank or a private investor, isn't going to invest their monies unless they know the numbers work, they know their potential ROI (return on investment), and they know if the business can service the debt. The funder will also want to be confident that the business owner understands the numbers. Do you understand yours?

Darcy Johnson, chief financial officer at Tormach Inc. and financial numbers guru, shares advice for new entrepreneurs:

Don't Go It Alone

If you are a new entrepreneur, seek advice and assistance from those who understand financials. If you can afford to hire an accountant, that's ideal. But if finances don't allow for that, think about family members or friends who know accounting and ask them to walk you through the numbers. If that's not an option, what about seeking out an accounting student or signing up for a beginner's accounting or QuickBooks course at your local community college? And, of course, there are a multitude of online resources to help familiarize you with profit and loss statements, balance sheets, cost versus accrual, and much more. The bottom line is this: know what the numbers mean!

> *The bottom line is this: know what the numbers mean!*

Understand Your Costs and Vet Your Data

When starting a new business, it's exciting to think of the thousands (or maybe millions) of dollars you are going to make. Before you can confidently say, "I'm going to sell $X worth of product this year," you must understand the cost to sell that amount. An entrepreneur who plans on selling $2 million worth of product with only a $10,000 investment probably doesn't understand their numbers or have a realistic plan to reach that number. A mentor or advisor can help you determine if your goal/projections are valid. Have you included *all* costs?

WHAT'S THE COST OF A PIZZA?

A restaurant that makes and sells pizza needs to determine how much each pizza costs to make. The most obvious is the cost of the ingredients, but what about the shipping costs associated with those ingredients and the cost of the oven and the cost to heat that oven? The owner must also pay someone to make and serve the pizza. What is that labor cost, including payroll taxes and paid leave time, to make each pizza? And what about the boxes for the to-go pizzas and the plates and utensils for dine-in customers? And let's not forget the cost of spoilage of the materials that are in excess of each pizza produced. There's more to the cost of pizza than you thought, isn't there? Once you've determined your true cost for every product and service, you can then determine what your selling price should be for your business to be profitable. With that information, you are able to forecast your expenses and income for the year. So, how many pizzas would you need to sell a year to make a profit?

Will you have to rent office, retail, or manufacturing space? How much labor will you need to hire? What are your material and supply chain costs? If you mapped out your business plan last year, are those numbers still accurate?

Your advisor can also help aid in determining or confirming your marketing plan. How will you reach your target audience, and how much will it cost? What's your business's budget for the upcoming year, and is it based in reality? Having someone experienced in business who can play devil's advocate will help ground the eager and enthusiastic new entrepreneur in reality, which is where banks and investors live.

Track Your Numbers

You can't know your numbers unless you track them, right? Develop a system for tracking all your income and expenses, and then *remember to consistently input your numbers into that system*! In the beginning, this can be as simple as an Excel spreadsheet. There are also some basic accounting software programs to get you started that are reasonably priced and will also help you forecast your income and expenses.

Key Financial Metrics

There are a lot of areas to focus on when starting a new business, and it can be easy to get stuck in the weeds and lose sight of the big picture and miss the warning signs. After all, as a start-up, you're scrambling for every penny, trying to make it go as far as it can while continually trying to adapt your business to the current market and economic trends so you will be ready to pivot when necessary. Here are key metrics to watch closely that will enable you to see trouble or opportunity before it's too late:

Cash Is King

Every business, at a minimum, must maintain enough cash to cover its existing debt and to decide when it's viable to incur new debt. For that to happen, every business must know their *real* cash number. If you only have $1,000 in the bank and no definitive new financing or revenue coming in, you can't commit to a $100,000 or even a $5,000 purchase order, no matter how badly you need the supplies to make more product.

As we learned in Bill's story, the cash that is sitting in your checking account does not reflect your available cash. To know how much available cash you have, you must understand how much debt you have, what the terms of that debt are, and if you can service it. Let's say a family member loans you $10,000 at 2 percent interest, and you don't need to begin paying back the loan for twenty-four months; you need to understand how that will affect your cash balance when the loan comes due and establish a revenue plan so you can repay it according to the terms agreed to. It's critical that you balance your company's cash and debt to make sure your equity is positive.

Always, always, always keep your personal and business monies separate right from the start. Comingling business and personal funds will blind you to the business's true cash balance and will be extremely difficult to disentangle as your business grows.

Gross Profit Margin

A business's gross profit margin is the revenue that remains after all cost of goods sold (COGS) has been subtracted, and it is one of the most important metrics you need to track for your business. So, what is COGS?

To know how much available cash you have, you must understand how much debt you have, what the terms of that debt are, and if you can service it.

It is the total of all expenses *directly related* to creating or acquiring the goods you sell. If you manufacture a product, your business's COGS would include expenses like materials and direct labor to make the product, package it, and transport the product to market. What it does not include are expenses such as rent, taxes, and utilities.

Once you have determined your current gross profit margin, set a reasonable goal to increase it over time and then keep your eye on it. Did you plan for a 40 percent margin, but over the last six months you've come out at 20 percent? If so, investigate the numbers to determine why. Are you capturing the right numbers, or did you include expenses that are not attributable to COGS? Is your gross profit margin fluctuating—40 percent one month and 10 percent the next? Then it's time to investigate your numbers again. Did a cost of production go up that wasn't projected for? Are your numbers allocated to the correct time period?

Your gross profit margin is the first telltale sign of an increase or decrease in your business's financial health. If you do not have a healthy profit margin, how will you pay all your non-COGS expenses like taxes, licenses, salaries, and insurance? How will you purchase materials and supplies for the future, and how will you make a living?

Cash versus Accrual Accounting

The cash accounting method is the simpler of the two. It is the recording of income and expenses in real time. If you have ordered supplies on January 1 that you will pay for on February 15, it will be recorded as a February expense. The same holds true for income. You may invoice a customer February 1, but you may not receive payment until March 15. In cash accounting, this income would be attributed to March.

This method always provides you real-time cash on hand. What it doesn't do is inform you of that "cash on hand" that may already be committed elsewhere at a future date, which can be misleading. Cash accounting does not meet the Generally Accepted Accounting Principles (GAAP). The GAAP are the standard framework of rules and guidelines that accountants must adhere to when preparing a business's financial statements in the United States.

With the accrual accounting method, income and expenses are recorded when they're billed and earned, regardless of when the money is actually received or paid out. In the examples above, the supplies ordered in January and the income invoiced in February would be recorded as expenses and income in those months: accounts payable and accounts receivable. In this way, accrual accounting provides a true representation of a business's income and expenses in a correctly timed sequence, providing you a more accurate financial picture of where you are and where you are going.

Percolating for Profits

One of my University of Wisconsin entrepreneur students, Ryan Mason, was determined to start his own business. He loved coffee, was an experienced barista, and believed that there was room in his college town for a coffee shop that produced really good coffee.

The day we started selling food in the coffee shop, our sales jumped 30 percent. It was an instant pop in revenue, which was great, because I'd been struggling to keep the business afloat for over six years before I finally realized I needed to make a drastic change. For the first several years, I was shifting money around a lot, kind of a "robbing Peter to pay Paul" type of thing. Which meant there wasn't any money left at the end of the day. After a while, I wasn't really enjoying the work, and I wasn't reaping rewards from the labors of my work.

Ryan Mason

When I look back to the beginning, I was confident early on because right off the bat I hit the sales targets I had set for the business. My initial success led me to believe that if I just kept doing what I was doing, revenues would climb like a hockey stick, and I'd be rich and famous.

Then summer hit, and the bulk of my customers went home for summer break. Our sales dropped 40 percent overnight. Personally, I didn't have much money, and the business hadn't yet built up any profits or savings. I did have a line of credit, and I started pushing off a lot of my payment terms with my vendors and just concentrated on paying immediate bills like rent and utilities. That helped me last through summer, and then once the fall hit, our sales immediately bounced back up.

There continued to be times when there wasn't much money in the bank, and when there was money in the bank, I knew I needed to save that to make it through the hard times—school breaks. I needed to do more. I opened the coffee shop serving only very traditional coffees. I wanted to serve espressos and cappuccinos, and it turned out that traditional coffee drinkers were a finite group. It just wasn't what the majority of the students were into. So, when I started looking at my numbers and profitability, I asked myself, "What are we really good at?" And that was espresso preparation. My next question was, "How can I use that to make more money?"

We started developing a lot of signature espresso and cappuccino drinks that appealed to a wider group of students, and then it was fun again. A cappuccino is very traditional, but if you add some chocolate or raspberry and a special name, nontraditional coffee drinkers are going to focus on that flavor that is familiar and that they like and be more open to the coffee it's in. We also began offering bakery items.

Changing the menu and increasing prices increased the coffee shop's profits, and I was able to catch up on all my old bills. The business stayed at a breakeven point for a few years, but just breaking even was no longer enough, and I knew I needed to do something drastic to change the trajectory of the profitability if the business was going to survive. There are three books that helped me understand business financials and ultimately scale my business:

- *Scaling Up: How a Few Companies Make It ... and Why the Rest Don't (Mastering the Rockefeller Habits 2.0)*, by Verne Harnish

- *Confronting Reality: Doing What Matters to Get Things Right*, by Larry Bossidy and Ram Charan

- *Simple Numbers, Straight Talk, Big Profits*, by Greg Crabtree

Based on the knowledge gained from these books, I created spreadsheets early on that enabled me to clearly see what had worked, what hadn't, and the ebb and flow of my revenue and expenses. Now it was time to drill down into the expenses that I had and see where I was spending money, how I was spending money, and also project what I expected to make in a month and what behaviors I needed to adopt in order to make the money I wanted to make.

After reviewing the numbers and my options, I decided to add food to the menu.

To move forward with adding food to the menu, Ryan needed a grease trap that was not within his budget. He lamented his problem to a local customer, who offered to pay for half the cost of a grease trap and receive coffee credits in return. He decided to go for it. The first day the coffee shop served food, sales increased by 30 percent, making the business profitable. Ryan is not an accountant, but by learning what the numbers mean and how they impact his business, he was able to make sound financial decisions that resulted in not only increasing profitability to the coffee shop but also leveraging that success to expand into event catering and coffee kiosks for festivals.

We've covered the essentials of starting and succeeding as an entrepreneur, but everyone can use a little help along the way. I strongly believe in mentors, and I'll share why in the next chapter.

Points to Remember

→ Seek accounting/financial advice before you get started. If you can't afford to hire an accountant, seek out those who may assist you in your family-and-friend circle and research organizations like the SBA or your school who may be able to offer assistance in these areas.

→ Know your numbers. How? By reviewing your financial statements at a minimum of once per month.

→ Validate your costs and projected sales.

→ Monitor key metrics that will enable you to see trouble or opportunity before it's too late: know your *real* cash number and your gross profit margin.

Recommended Resources:

- *Scaling Up: How a Few Companies Make It ... and Why the Rest Don't (Mastering the Rockefeller Habits 2.0),* by Verne Harnish

- *Confronting Reality: Doing What Matters to Get Things Right,* by Larry Bossidy and Ram Charan

- *Simple Numbers, Straight Talk, Big Profits,* by Greg Crabtrce

- Sample Financial Statements in Appendix A

- Sample Statement of Forecast Assumptions in Appendix B

- Statement of Forecast Assumptions Template in Appendix C

- Interactive Financial Statements Template, found on my website www.jameshhunter.com.

CHAPTER 10

THE IMPORTANCE OF A MENTOR

Most kids have a lemonade stand at some point in their childhood. Baily Paxton was no different, except before that lemonade stand, he had a golf ball stand. He discovered the opportunity when he would visit his grandmother's farm in Grand Rapids, Michigan.

My grandmother had a field that ran parallel to a golf course, and the golfers would hit their golf balls over the barbed wire fence that separated the field from the course. It was like an Easter egg hunt every time we'd go visit. I'd collect all the balls and then sell them back to the golfers. I didn't make a lot of money, but I did make some. That was my first "business" as a kid, but it wasn't my last.

Growing up, I was surrounded by the entrepreneurial spirit. My dad was always entrepreneurial, and one of our good family friends, John Wechsler (founder of Formstack and

Launch Fishers), was an entrepreneur. When I was in the eighth grade, my dad decided he wanted to either buy or start his own business. That was a cool process to go through with him. It was right when Shark Tank came out, and my dad and I would talk out different ideas.

Baily Paxton

When I was in high school, we moved from Indiana to Michigan, and every summer I would intern at Launch Fishers in Indianapolis. Shadowing John and observing his entrepreneurial endeavors was a great opportunity. In my freshman year of high school, my dad bought three Right at Home franchises (a home care company). During the school year, I would always fill in shifts as needed while learning about the business.

The summer before my senior year in high school, I attended the Teen Entrepreneurship Academy in Irvine, California. I had an idea for a product and worked all week long to develop a business plan around it. The goal of the business was to identify, redesign, and market medical devices with expired patents. I pitched the product idea and won the competition.

I know not everyone is fortunate enough to have such unfettered access to entrepreneurial mentors as Baily did, but that doesn't mean one or two aren't out there for you! You just need to look for them. Baily found additional mentors to learn from by tapping into available resources.

As a senior in high school, he agonized over which college to attend. Since his family now lived in Michigan, the least expensive solution was to attend Michigan State University. One aspect of Michigan State University that was attractive to Baily was Spartan Innovations (SI).

When I made my initial campus visit to MSU, I met with Paul Jakes, who is the director of the SI program. Knowing Paul when I arrived to start classes was great. Connecting with a mentor right away enabled me to get heavily involved with the entrepreneurial program with my first company from day one.

SI is a wholly owned subsidiary of the Michigan State University Foundation (MSUF).[18] *SI's objective is to help drive MSU entrepreneurs to "develop their ideas, create business plans, and successfully launch highly technical businesses. SI sources its inventions through its close relationship with MSU Technologies, the technology transfer arm of Michigan State University, which receives 175–200 unique invention disclosures every year from MSU faculty." This close collaboration provides SI the opportunity to "identify and nurture early-stage technologies that could serve as the foundation for a new venture."*

---

18 "Venture Creation," Michigan State University Foundation, accessed January 2022, https://www.msufoundation.org/venture-creation.

Michigan State is not alone in offering innovative programs for college entrepreneurs. These types of programs are replicated throughout colleges and universities across the US. Cast a wide net when searching for collegiate entrepreneurial opportunities.

Baily took advantage of the resources offered through SI. Through this support organization, he developed AgileCare Solutions. This app-based company offered a solution for families, caregivers, and organizations to easily schedule tasks; set alerts; log vitals, mood, and daily activities; and share notes—all with a few simple taps. It uses predictive analytics and artificial intelligence to provide preventative health insights and drive real-time care, and it allows caregivers anywhere to communicate and collaborate with each other. It also provides a daily task and wellness tracker that uses icons to keep information consistent and continuous among caregivers.

AgileCare Solutions was named one of the 2019 Best Tech Startups in East Lansing by the *Tech Tribune*. Each year the *Tech Tribune* staff compiles the very best tech start-ups in East Lansing, Michigan. In doing their research, they consider several factors, including but not limited to the following:

- Revenue potential

- Leadership team

- Brand/product traction

- Competitive landscape

Additionally, all companies must be independent (unacquired), privately owned, at most ten years old, and have received at least one round of funding to qualify.

Baily had mentors that offered entrepreneurship experience from eighth grade through college, and he engaged in organized competition and selected a university with strong student entrepreneurship support. It is no wonder that he pursued entrepreneurship and was successful at it. Baily is currently a Global Innovation Fellow at the Henry Ford Health Institute.

So, what should you look for in an entrepreneurial mentor, and where can you find them?

The Right Mentor

My first mentor was a tough old guy. The company I took over at that time failed, but my mentor taught me significant lessons that I still utilize today. In business there are partners, investors, and a variety of stakeholders, and as the founder/CEO, you need to be able to figure out a deal structure that balances the interests of all the parties involved. At the time, I had no idea what the possibilities were, but my mentor had so much experience that he could come up with viable suggestions off the top of his head. I listened and I learned.

I had worked in big companies that didn't offer the opportunity to be creative. You just did what you were supposed to do. So, when I got into my own business for the first time, I had to learn how to create solutions in which all parties had their interests covered and were protected: I had to be able to see the perspective of all parties involved and understand the balance of power. That was an invaluable

In business there are partners, investors, and a variety of stakeholders, and as the founder/CEO, you need to be able to figure out a deal structure that balances the interests of all the parties involved.

lesson for me to learn early on. My mentor also ran interference for me. When a customer or creditor was taking advantage, he would intervene and set things straight. Eventually, I gained the knowledge and confidence to recognize those situations and stand up for myself.

Now I am the one with many years of experience that I am eager to share. If I can help a new entrepreneur be more prepared than I was, so that although they will experience failure, it won't be as catastrophic as mine, I'm happy to do so. The other reason I am motivated by mentoring is that I believe in the free-market system that is fostered in this country. America has something good that we need to preserve, and I believe the more people who understand that and are able to take advantage of the opportunity, the stronger the country will be. It is during your college years that you will have the most opportunities to take advantage of free entrepreneurial resources.

The importance of a mentor cannot be overstated. Kabbage, Inc., a global financial services, technology, and data platform serving small businesses, surveyed more than two hundred small businesses throughout the US to understand the importance of mentorship to small business owners. Here's what it showed:[19]

- Only 22 percent of small business owners had mentors when they started their business.

- Only 17 percent indicated they have an advisor, which suggests a paid relationship for consulting and advice.

- A whopping 92 percent agree that mentors have a direct impact on growth and the survival of their business.

- Interestingly, 61 percent of small business owners mentor others, and **58 percent specifically mentor younger entrepreneurs.**

---

19   Kabbage, "Data Shows Mentors are Vital to Small Business Success," accessed April 2022, https://www.kabbage.com/resource-center/grow/data-shows-mentors-are-vital-to-small-business-success/.

"A great mentor is someone who provides objective advice, provides counsel from a fresh perspective, is willing to collaborate, listen and learn, as well as remind you of your goals, your purpose, and what you're working so hard to achieve," says Amy Zimmerman, head of people operations at Kabbage.

Kabbage's report shows the willingness of small business owners to mentor young entrepreneurs (58 percent!); you just need to reach out to them. If there are local business owners whom you admire and/or know, pick up the phone and call them. Even if they are not the right mentor for you, they may direct you to someone who is.

CHARACTERISTICS OF A STRONG MENTOR

I introduced SCORE (Service Corps of Retired Executives) in chapter 1 and want to highlight the key characteristics they look for in their volunteer mentors:

The ability to …

- stop and suspend judgment,

- listen and learn,

- assess and analyze,

- test ideas and teach with tools, and

- set expectations and encourage the dream.

Whether you find a mentor in a family member, friend, organizations like SCORE, or through school, it's important to vet them to ensure they are the right mentor for you. Think about the list above, and determine if the person you are thinking of asking to mentor you or is already serving as your mentor meets those qualifications.

SCORE can be beneficial to a new business owner. Within the first year of one of my recent start-ups, I obtained a government-backed loan. It was called a "patriot loan" since I was a veteran. It provided $50,000 of general funding that helped launch the business in the first six months of operation. One of the loan requirements was that I was to team up with a SCORE volunteer to give me advice. The requirement was for at least two meetings with the SCORE volunteer. I held these meetings and appreciated the SCORE volunteer taking time to meet with me. However, I found that the SCORE volunteer had considerably less entrepreneurial experience than I did. At that point in the development of the business, I was not seeking general business mentorship (although any entrepreneur can use seasoned advice). The point is that mentorship is really important and must be targeted to the needs of the entrepreneur.

I also recommend adding to that list that they have experience in your business sector or a related sector. While it's not a deal breaker if they don't, it is significantly beneficial if they do. They should also have a clear understanding of the ownership structures we discussed in chapter 8, "Understanding Legal and Tax Issues," and the financial statements discussed in chapter 9, "Mastering the Numbers." Finally, do you trust them and feel supported by them? What is your gut telling you? If you begin working with a mentor and it just doesn't feel right, take a step back and reassess.

- Are they giving advice that doesn't make sense?

- Are they telling you what you should do rather than helping you work through solutions?

- Do they have less experience than they originally indicated?

- Do you feel good about the relationship?

If you don't feel good about the experience and aren't learning, it's okay to end the mentorship. After all, the purpose is to help you learn and move forward, and if that's not happening, it's time to look for a new mentor.

Points to Remember

- ➡ Strong mentors have the ability to stop and suspend judgment, listen and learn, assess and analyze, test ideas and teach with tools, set expectations, and encourage your dream.

- ➡ If you don't feel good about the experience and aren't learning, it's okay to end the mentorship.

- ➡ Mentors are out there—you just need to look for them: 61 percent of small business owners mentor others, and **58 percent specifically mentor younger entrepreneurs.**

- ➡ Connect with entrepreneurial organizations through your school to network and meet your potential mentor.

Recommended Resources:

- ➡ SCORE, https://www.score.org/content/mission-vision-and-values

- ➡ Spartan Innovations, https://www.msufoundation.org/venture-creation

- ➡ Future Founders, https://www.futurefounders.com/about-us/

- ➡ Junior Achievement USA, serving students elementary through high school, https://jausa.ja.org/programs/index

➡ LinkedIn

1. **Use hashtags** in LinkedIn's search box. The social plat-form's support team suggests using hashtags such as #OfferHelp, #Careeradvice, or #Mentorship.

2. Join **mentorship groups** on LinkedIn. You can find these groups by using the previously mentioned hashtags or by doing searches in LinkedIn using other relevant words such as *community* or *advice*.

CHAPTER 11

ETHICS: DOING THE RIGHT THING

For me personally, the most challenging ethical dilemmas surround the decision of whether or not to let an employee go. On the one hand, you want to make sure that the work being done supports the organization and its mission and that everyone is treating customers and other employees properly—this is critical. On the other hand, you also want to make sure you're treating the individual involved properly. This is where it gets tough, because what's best for the organization may not be best for the individual, and vice versa. Even when you want the best for the individual employee, the reality is that keeping them in a situation where they are not appropriately producing for the organization is not good for them in the long run.

I had an employee who was smart and hardworking, but he struggled to finish anything. He would just keep working at the same thing repeatedly but achieving no end product. We had him take a personality test to see where he might best fit in the company. The result of the test was that there was no position in our organization that he was suited for. Not being able to find the right job for him bothered me a lot. I did try everything I could, but it's difficult for me to have to part ways with someone I am working with who is trying to do a good job. In this case, keeping him on was not in the best interest of the company.

You must weigh the impact on the organization and ensure that the organization is properly managed while also considering the individual. These types of decisions should be made sooner rather than later. Too often, difficult employee situations are repeatedly postponed until they become so detrimental to the company that the organization is forced to fire—that scenario is bad for the individual and the organization.

Economic and Legal Considerations

It would be difficult to find a sound ethical solution to a business dilemma without considering its economic and legal ramifications. How much will the solution cost? Cost is not just factoring the cash output—you must also factor in the time and energy involved in potential audits, legal proceedings, and the like. And what about customer defections, a tarnished reputation, and employee turnover? These, too, have significant costs associated with them.

What about your legal rights and responsibilities? Is pursuing a legal path, even when you are on the right side of the law, always the best solution? If you win a long and drawn-out court battle at the cost of three to four years of zero growth because you didn't have the bandwidth to fight your case *and* strategize for growth—was that the best solution for the company? It all depends on what's at stake and what the values of your company are.

These decisions should not be made in a vacuum—engage legal and financial professionals, stakeholders, and advisors as appropriate throughout the decision-making process.

Getting It Right

Darcy Johnson, the financial guru I introduced in chapter 9, is also a wonderful example of how to set the bar for high ethical standards and how to inspire everyone to meet those standards. With a BA in accounting and finance from Lakeland University and an MBA from Keller School of Management, Darcy was well suited for her position of finance director for Dynamic Solutions Worldwide, LLC (Dynatrap).

Darcy's finance director position with Dynatrap entailed not only full responsibility for all accounting and finance functions but also responsibility for information technology and human resources. The business was a small one but grew from $12 million in sales to well over $40 million during Darcy's tenure. She was instrumental in creating the positive culture that existed within the organization. Certainly the top management of the company had ultimate responsibility for the culture and could be described as the morale officers of the business. However, the pervasive nature of the positive culture achieved at Dynatrap was as much Darcy's doing as it was the actions of top management.

Dynatrap was an entrepreneurial effort. As CEO and majority owner, I formed an LLC along with two minority owners. The three of us worked together to buy a product name and customer list from a bank that was handling a bankruptcy. It was a bootstrap effort, with two of the owners investing modest amounts into equity and the CEO investing over $100,000 in loans to the business. Banks would not consider loaning to the business until it had been operating for at least two years. Fortunately, a patriot loan for $50,000 was obtained (the CEO was a veteran), and a nontraditional lender provided a loan of $85,000. These two outside loans and continual loans from the CEO and his family members got the company to the two-year point at which banks would start lending. The bootstrap nature of the business continued in its early years until profits amassed sufficient equity to attract a major lender, JPMorgan Chase Bank, N.A.

> Bootstrapping is a process whereby an entrepreneur starts a self-sustaining business, markets it, and grows the business by using limited resources or money. This is accomplished without the use of venture capital firms or even significant angel investment. [20]

Darcy was instrumental in working out arrangements with the Chase Bank, and she administered the day-to-day relationships. In the second year of Darcy's tenure, Dynatrap management decided to engage in long-range planning. The facilitator for this process was René Boer, certified EOS Implementer, author of *How to Be a Great Boss*, and speaker. This effort was not only for planning the company's future but also involved setting some philosophical foundations for the management of the company. René nurtured the management group to create a statement of core values:

- We are Dynapreneurs—we get things done regardless of the obstacles.

- We run with a high motor—we don't give up until the job is done.

---

20   Ian Harvey, "Companies That Succeeded with Bootstrapping," Investopedia, June 8, 2021, https://www.investopedia.com/articles/investing/082814/companies-succeeded-bootstrapping.asp#bootstrapping-a-businesscompany.

- We do the right thing—we don't take the easy way out with customers, suppliers, our team members, or the community; it must be right, or we don't do it.

- We have a positive mental attitude—we believe that "can do" is the answer to problems as they arise; every customer should leave happy.

Darcy was the person who nurtured the team and was the main catalyst that made the company a great place to work, earning Dynatrap the designation of "Great Place to Work in 2017–2018."

Here are some of the ways that Darcy led the company culture:

Darcy organized regular team-building events for all employees, including

- A picnic with beanbag-tossing championship,

- lunch with game competition,

- escape room interactive adventure games,

- holiday lunches (employees drew names for presents, and everyone engaged in team-competitive games), and

- inflatable money machines.

Every employee was recognized as a valuable member of the team. Management understood that the company's high profits were a result of the hard work of all their employees. Dynatrap's policy for setting salaries was to compare job specifications with other jobs in the community and to pay at least 5 percent more than similar jobs. An incentive plan was installed, and all employees earned a bonus when the company achieved the profit plan each month. The greater the profit in excess of plan, the greater the bonus. When employees are directly compensated and acknowledged for their role in the success of a company, they are willing to stick it out and work even harder during times of lower profits. The profit and loss statement was available for all employees to review.

Darcy stood as an example of how an organization can be run with true appreciation for the contribution of each employee. The strong efforts of Darcy to make the work environment enjoyable for employees was important. However, the top management members had to embody sound ethical management, or no efforts by Darcy would have been effective. She had the full backing of top management, and that support completed the environment needed.

Ethical Business

What is ethical business? This question is answered simply: praiseworthy business is based upon cooperation, voluntary exchange, partnership, and association. Unacceptable business is based upon extraction, theft, slavery, imperialism, colonization, and fraud. These definitions are put forth by Dr. James R. Otteson, faculty director at the Deloitte Center for Ethical Leadership at the University of Notre Dame's Mendoza College of Business. Dr. Otteson points out that real wealth in inflation-adjusted terms has been constant at $1 to $3 per person per day for the hundred thousand years up to the year 1800. From that point forward to today, real wealth has increased in the world to $48 per person per day and to $164 per person per day in the US. Dr. Otteson postulates that the increase in wealth has occurred due to the prevalence of free market economics that has come to flower throughout the world, led especially in the US. Dr. Otteson discusses this and related topics in the book *Actual Ethics*.

While it can be argued that some entrepreneurs operate in an unethical manner, the greatest satisfaction for successful entrepreneurs is achieving "win-win" results where customers, employees, and entrepreneurs achieve the satisfaction of providing a product or service of value to customers while giving beneficial employment and achieving a profitable result to compensate owners for the investment risk they have undertaken. The resulting free market economy has propelled our country to unprecedented economic success with economic benefits for participants in our economy.

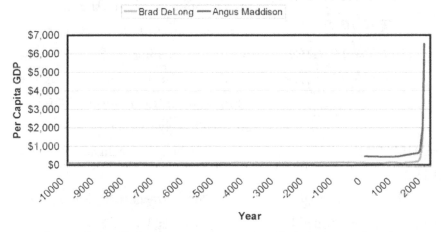

World Per Capita GDP
10000 BCE - 2003 CE (1990 International Dollars)

Source: J. Bradford DeLong, "Estimating World GDP, One Million B.C.– Present," http://holtz.org/Library/Social%20Science/Economics/Estimating%20 World%20GDP%20by%20DeLong/Estimating%20World%20GDP.htm.

Actual Ethics, by Dr. Otteson, is a book about how you should live. It presents a concise presentation of fundamental principles applied to currently important moral and political topics. The book discusses judgment as requiring freedom and responsibility. Good judgment develops not only by enjoying the freedom to exercise it but also being required to take responsibility for its exercise.

Dr. Otteson's book emphasizes the importance of freedom to exercise decision-making but also of experiencing the results of this freedom and accepting the consequences. To the extent that this freedom in decision-making is significant, the economic results are striking. The *Economic Freedom of the World* reports annually on what kind of government is most conducive to material prosperity.

> *Good judgment develops not only by enjoying the freedom to exercise it but also being required to take responsibility for its exercise.*

The most recent comprehensive data available from the *Economic Freedom of the World* is from 2019.[21] Hong Kong remains in the top position in economic freedom. The apparent increased insecurity of property rights and the weakening of the rule of law caused by the interventions of the Chinese government during 2020 and 2021 will likely have a negative impact on Hong Kong's score, especially in area 2, "Legal System and Property Rights," going forward.

Singapore once again comes in second. The next-highest-scoring nations are New Zealand, Switzerland, Georgia, United States, Ireland, Lithuania, Australia, and Denmark.

Rankings of Other Major Countries

The rankings of some other major countries are as follows: Canada (14th), Japan (18th), Germany (22nd), Italy (47th), France (53rd), Mexico (75th), Russia (100th), India (108th), Brazil (109th), and China (116th).

---

21   Fraser Institute—Economic Freedom, "Economic Freedom of North America 2021," accessed November 2021, https://www.fraserinstitute.org/studies/economic-freedom.

Ten Lowest-Rated Countries

The ten lowest-rated countries are Central African Republic, Democratic Republic of Congo, Syria, Republic of Congo, Iran, Zimbabwe, Algeria, Libya, Sudan, and lastly Venezuela.

Nations That Are Economically Free
Outperform Nonfree Nations in Indicators of Well-Being

- Nations in the top quartile of economic freedom had an average per-capita GDP of $50,619 in 2019, compared to $5,911 for nations in the bottom quartile (PPP constant 2017 international $).

- In the top quartile, the average income of the poorest 10 percent was $14,400, compared to $1,549 in the bottom quartile (PPP constant 2017 international $). Interestingly, the average income of the poorest 10 percent in the most economically free nations is more than twice the average per-capita income in the least-free nations.

- In the top quartile, 0.9 percent of the population experience extreme poverty (US$1.90 a day) compared to 34.1 percent in the lowest quartile.

- Life expectancy is 81.1 years in the top quartile compared to 65.9 years in the bottom quartile.

These statistics show that the well-being of citizens is related to the size and intervention of government. As discussed in *Actual Ethics,* what government we allow to exist has a strong influence on our personal ethics—how we exercise our decision-making and how we accept the results of our decisions.

Guiding Principles or Points to Ponder

A physician shall be dedicated to providing competent medical care, with compassion and respect for human dignity and rights.[22]

A lawyer shall not represent a client if the representation involves a concurrent conflict of interest.[23]

Social workers may disclose confidential information when appropriate with valid consent from a client or a person legally authorized to consent on behalf of a client.[24]

Even with these ethical standards in place, there is room for misinterpretation based on an individual's personal morals and values. What one person determines to be *compassionate* and *respectful* care may look widely different from another's perspective. Determining when it is *appropriate* to disclose confidential information is not black and white for everyone. So, if gray areas exist even in those professions that are provided a code of ethics, how do business owners presume to make the right decision when ethical dilemmas arise?

In their textbook, *Entrepreneurial Small Business*, Jerome Katz and Richard Green offer guidance for navigating the challenges of ethical dilemmas. Based on their book and my own experience, I offer the following insights.

---

22   American Medical Association, "AMA Code of Medical Ethics," revised June 2001, accessed January 2022, https://www.ama-assn.org/sites/ama-assn.org/files/corp/media-browser/principles-of-medical-ethics.pdf.

23   ABA Journal, "Rule 1.7: Conflict of Interest: Current Clients," accessed October 2021, https://www.americanbar.org/groups/professional_responsibility/publications/model_rules_of_professional_conduct/rule_1_7_conflict_of_interest_current_clients/.

24   National Association of Social Workers, "Read the Code of Ethics," accessed October 2021, https://www.socialworkers.org/About/Ethics/Code-of-Ethics/Code-of-Ethics-English.

When faced with an ethical decision, one should first clearly state what the moral issue is.

Merriam-Webster defines the difference between morals and ethics as follows:

Morals often describes one's particular values concerning what is right and what is wrong. While *ethics* can refer broadly to moral principles, one often sees it applied to questions of correct behavior within a relatively narrow area of activity.

In addition, *morals* usually connotes an element of subjective preference while *ethics* tends to suggest aspects of universal fairness and the question of whether or not an action is responsible.

Next, one should determine the relevant alternative solutions to the ethical problem. Finally, one should determine the alternative that best represents the proper solution that they can live with and then implement that solution.

There are questions that you must ask when faced with a moral problem:

- Who will be hurt by my decision, and how severe will the hurt be?

- Who will benefit, and how much will the benefit be compared to the hurt that the decision may cause?

- As a result of my decision, what will be my obligations to others?

- As a result of my decision, what are the obligations of others to me, and will these obligations of others help me carry out my decision?

Below are four proven philosophies to try when solving an ethical dilemma:[25]

1. **Golden rule:** Am I treating the other party the way I would like to be treated?

2. **Utilitarianism:** Would my decision result in the best situation for the most people over the long term?

3. **Universalism:** What if everyone treated everyone else in the same way that I would be treating them?

4. **Billboard principle:** What if everyone everywhere could be aware of my decision? Would I be proud of my decision?

We are all faced with ethical dilemmas in our day-to-day lives that we may not even consider.

*   You return home from shopping to discover an item in your bag that the clerk didn't charge you for. What do you do? Keep it because it wasn't your fault, or go back to the store and pay for it?

*   You back out of a parking space and lightly bump the car behind you. No one sees, and the damage is a small dent. What do you do? Pull away quickly before someone does see, or leave a note for the owner of the car you hit?

*   You have the last-minute opportunity to spend the day with an old friend you haven't seen in a while. You are out of vacation time, but you do still have sick time on the books. You know your team is already short staffed today. What do you do? Feign illness and spend the day hanging out with your friend, or go to work and miss the opportunity to reconnect with your

---

25   Jerome Katz and Richard Green, *Entrepreneurial Small Business* (New York City: McGraw-Hill Education, 2018): 72.

friend? Now, think of that same scenario where you are the employer and your employee falsely called out sick knowing the team was short staffed. How would you handle that?

Take a moment to notice when these small dilemmas come up for you or those around you, and apply the four philosophies above to help find a solution that works for you. This will help you to see a new perspective and begin to prepare you for the ethical dilemmas that come your way in business.

Points to Remember

➡ Establish ongoing processes to show your employees that you value them.

➡ Develop a set of core values for your company and make sure all employees are aware of them and understand their responsibility in carrying them out.

➡ Carefully evaluate all potential solutions to an ethical dilemma, and involve appropriate legal and financial professionals, stakeholders, and advisors in the process.

➡ Once the appropriate solution is determined, take action to implement it.

Recommended Resources:

➡ *Actual Ethics*, by James R. Otteson

➡ *Entrepreneurial Small Business*, by Jerome Katz and Richard Green

CONCLUSION

I hope *Graduate a CEO* has inspired you to seriously consider all your entrepreneurial possibilities and all the incredible resources available to you as a college student. I encourage you to use this book as a guide throughout your entrepreneurial journey. Refer to it often, filling it with highlights, notes, and bookmarks as you enter each new phase of your business's development. I have recommended several excellent business books, but there are many more out there. Read as many as you can—learning from the successes and failures of others is invaluable to the aspiring entrepreneur.

Through the student stories, you have heard firsthand of the challenges and rewards of young entrepreneurship and what it takes to be an entrepreneur. Do you have what it takes? Now's the time to find out. Assess your traits, skills, strengths, and weaknesses. You won't have all the requirements of an entrepreneur, but the good news is, you don't have to. Access as many entrepreneurial resources you can through your school, business organizations, and personal and professional connections and affiliations. Remember, mentors and opportunities are everywhere; you just need to seek them out.

Sam Padilla Castro, entrepreneurial student and founder of Steven Mentors, is a big believer in accessing mentors and resources through networking.

I think the best mentoring relationships come naturally, and for that to happen you have to connect with a wide variety of organizations and people. Josh (fellow student entrepreneur) became a mentor to me after we started

hanging out and talking about business, and it naturally happened. When I entered the Future Founders program, they became my mentors, and the program connected me with local business owners who also evolved

Sam Padilla Castro

into mentors for me. One of the greatest entrepreneurial benefits my school provided was the financial support to attend conferences. The network that I was able to build from those opportunities provided me leadership, communication, and tech knowledge that you can't get in a classroom setting.

Matt Kemper, cofounder of Light Fruit Company, built his network and mentors through job experience. Matt intentionally changed jobs throughout high school and college so he could experience a variety of functional areas.

I've worked for over ten businesses over the course of the last eight years, and I really enjoy working for and learning from small business owners. My senior year in high school, I managed an ice cream shop, which exposed me to new aspects of the business. After that, I wanted to learn sales, so I sold shoes for a Midwest shoe retailer for two years. In college, I was a marketing and communications intern with

Matt Kemper

Principal Financial in Des Moines. They are a Fortune 500 company, and it was eye opening for me. It was one of my favorite experiences, because everything was so new to me and the company was so big in terms of accounts and projects.

As a business owner, you'll also need to connect with professional legal and tax advisors. It's never too early to seek professional counsel in this area. This is not a one-stop necessity; as your business evolves, so will your legal and tax needs. Seek guidance frequently.

Still feel like you are struggling to find ideas? I encourage you to give the IDEATE Method a try—you may find that you have more potential ideas than you realize! Once you have your idea, follow the process from visualizing and testing your big idea by mapping out your Business Canvas Model and diving into customer discovery.

Registered nurse and graduate student Lindsey Roddy hadn't thought of entrepreneurship, let alone considered whether she had an idea that could turn into a business. Then her professors asked, "So, Lindsey, what are your ideas?" and her whole world changed.

I had two professors who were innovators—one had created their own software, and the other had created a product—and one day they asked, "Lindsey, what are your ideas?" It wasn't long before I recalled a traumatic incident that had occurred with one of my patients. This patient had just gone through open heart surgery, and we were getting him

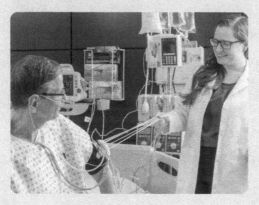

Lindsey Roddy

up and moving when the IV line that was going into his neck providing his life support medication got caught behind him and pulled out. I'll never forget my patient's face when he started to feel the effects of those meds being withdrawn, an incident that could have killed him. We had to do some emergency interventions and call the physicians back in, and while he was okay at the end of the day, I was not. It scared the heck out of me. When prompted for ideas by my professors, I thought, *There must be a way to keep this from happening."*

Critical care patients often require multiple (sometimes as many as twenty) IV tubes and wiring to connect them to necessary fluids, medications, and monitoring devices. Organizing and securing all this tubing and wiring can be challenging for both the patient and the medical staff, and as in the case of Lindsey's patient, it can be dangerous if they become tangled, pulled on, etc. In an attempt to make it more manageable, nurses often resort to their own makeshift solution of taping the lines together. When Lindsey shared the first drawings of her prototype to potentially solve this problem, her professors suggested she join the Student Startup Challenge through the Lubar Entrepreneurship Center at UWM.

> The Student Startup Challenge really was the beginning for me. I was the only nurse there, and I was fortunate that my PhD studies aligned with what would be the next step in my business development process—customer discovery through qualitative interviewing. We asked a lot of people a lot of questions to best understand the problem. Other people have tried to create a solution for this problem, but I don't think they did enough customer discovery, and they didn't do it in the way we did. We were on the ground all the time, continuously talking to people who were end users and the people who would be buying the product

The data gathered by Lindsey and her team enabled them to design a product that addressed the problems that clinicians reported over and over again: the need for mobility, versatility, and the ability to accommodate up to eight lines at a time. The data also provided funders the confidence they needed to invest in Lindsey's business. Lindsey's due diligence in her customer discovery has paid off. The

Secure*Move*-TLC™ is now FDA approved and, with the help of investors, is ready to go to market in 2022.

The process of customer discovery happens in tandem with knowing your numbers (Is your product financially viable?) and continual assessment of whether to pivot or persevere (Did you discover that what you thought was your customer's problem was something completely different? Should you pivot to developing a new product, or persevere and determine if there is another market for your current product?) Remember, the winning end product you sell will not be developed overnight—have patience and perseverance. Successful entrepreneurs like Eric Ries, Steve Blank, and Bob Dorf advocate for the minimum viable product process for good reason— heed their advice, and prepare to start selling!

Selling may be out of your comfort zone, but it's a job that must be done, and it's not just about selling your product or service. Before you can begin selling to customers, you must first *sell* your passion, confidence, knowledge, and business potential to prospective investors and supporters. This is where the development and presentation of a professional business plan will set you on a path to success.

You've collected and analyzed all the data to confirm you have a solid business idea. Business partners and stakeholders are on board. Now it's time to take a step back and ask, "Do the business prospects, my partners and stakeholders, my mentors, and my financials still *feel* right for me? Do I trust the plan and everyone involved?" If it does and you do, fantastic! It's time to pull the trigger. If it doesn't, determine what's not working and make the necessary changes. Trust and instinct are important components of being an

> *Trust and instinct are important components of being an entrepreneur.*

entrepreneur. Make the time throughout your entrepreneurial journey to listen, question, and learn so that as CEO, you can make informed decisions for you and your company.

Visit my website at www.jameshhunter.com for additional resources and for contact info. I'd love to hear from you!

Best of luck in your entrepreneurial adventures!

SAMPLE INCOME STATEMENT, BALANCE SHEET, AND STATEMENT OF CASH FLOWS

Sample Income Statement

www.jameshhunter.com

$ in 000's

	2023	2024	2025
	PROJ'D YR. 2022	PROJ'D YR. 2023	PROJ'D YR. 2024
REVENUE (SALES)	$91.0	$152.0	$652.1
REVENUE (OTHER)	$0.0	$0.0	$0.0
REVENUE (OTHER)	$0.0	$0.0	$0.0
REVENUE (OTHER)	$0.0	$0.0	$0.0
REVENUE (OTHER)	$0.0	$0.0	$0.0
TOTAL REVENUE	$91.0	$152.0	$652.1
TOTAL COST OF SALES	$0.0	$0.0	$0.0
NET GROSS MARGIN	$91.0	$152.0	$652.1
%			
SELL, GEN, & ADMIN EXPENSES			
Wages & Salaries	$4.8	$4.8	$4.8
Payroll Tax Expense	$1.2	$1.2	$1.2
Liability Insurance	$2.4	$2.4	$2.4
Phone, Internet, Website, Computer Expense	$1.2	$1.2	$1.2
Bank Service Fees	$0.0	$0.0	$0.0
Merchant Account Fees	$0.0	$0.0	$0.0
Rent Expense	$2.4	$2.4	$2.4
Depreciation	$0.0	$0.0	$0.0
Amortization	$1.2	$1.2	$1.2
Utilities Expense	$2.4	$2.4	$2.4
Office Supplies	$0.0	$0.0	$0.0
Advertising Expenses	$4.8	$10.0	$20.0
Legal & Accounting Expenses	$1.0	$0.0	$1.0
Licenses & Permits	$0.0	$0.0	$0.0
Rent	$0.0	$0.0	$0.0
Travel Expenses	$0.0	$0.0	$0.0
Miscellaneous	$0.0	$0.0	$0.0
TOTAL SELL, GEN, & ADMIN EXPENSES	$21.4	$25.6	$36.6
OPERATING INCOME	$69.6	$126.4	$615.5
OTHER INCOME/(EXPENSE)			
Interest Expense	$0.0	$0.0	$0.0
TOTAL OTHER INC. (EXP.)	$0.0	$0.0	$0.0
NET INCOME	$69.6	$126.4	$615.5

Sample Balance Sheet

www.jameshhunter.com

$ in 000's

	PROJECTED	PROJECTED	PROJECTED	PROJECTED
	12/31/22	12/31/23	12/31/24	12/31/25
ASSETS				
Current Assets				
Cash	$1.6	$39.8	$144.6	$565.6
Accounts Receivable	$0.0	$0.0	$0.0	$0.0
Inventory	$0.0	$0.0	$0.0	$0.0
Deposits	$0.0	$0.0	$0.0	$0.0
Prepaid Expense	$2.4	$2.4	$2.4	$2.4
Total Current Assets	$4.0	$42.2	$147.0	$568.0
FIXED ASSETS				
Fixed Assets at Cost	$0.0	$0.0	$0.0	$0.0
Less Accumulated Depreciation	$0.0	$0.0	$0.0	$0.0
Net Fixed Assets	$0.0	$0.0	$0.0	$0.0
OTHER ASSETS				
Intellectual Property	$6.0	$6.0	$6.0	$6.0
Less Accumulated Amortization	$0.0	$1.2	$2.4	$3.6
Net Other Assets	$6.0	$4.8	$3.6	$2.4
Total Assets	$10.0	$47.0	$150.6	$570.4
LIABILITIES & EQUITY				
Current Liabilities				
Accounts Payable	$0.0	$0.0	$0.0	$0.0
Accrued Expenses	$0.0	$0.2	$0.2	$0.2
Notes Payable - Bank (Cur. Por.)	$0.0	$0.0	$0.0	$0.0
Notes Payable - Bank LOC	$0.0	$0.0	$0.0	$0.0
Notes Payable - Owner	$0.0	$0.0	$0.0	$0.0
Notes Payable - Other	$0.0	$0.0	$0.0	$0.0
Total Current Liabilities	$0.0	$0.2	$0.2	$0.2
LONG TERM DEBT				
Notes Payable - Bank (Less Cur. Por.)	$0.0	$0.0	$0.0	$0.0
Total Liabilities	$0.0	$0.2	$0.2	$0.2
EQUITY				
Member Investment	$10.0	$5.0	$5.0	$5.0
Retained Earnings (Prev. Yr.)	$0.0	$0.0	$69.6	$196.0
Current Year Retained Earnings	$0.0	$69.6	$126.4	$615.4
Less Distributions to Members	$0.0	($27.84)	($50.56)	($246.16)
Total Equity	$10.0	$46.8	$150.4	$570.2
TOTAL LIABILITIES & EQUITY	$10.0	$47.0	$150.6	$570.4

Sample Statement of Cash Flows

www.jameshhunter.com

$ in 000's

	2023	2024	2025
	PROJ'D	PROJ'D	PROJ'D
	YR. 2023	YR. 2024	YR. 2025
Net Profit	$69.6	$126.4	$615.4
Add Back Depreciation	$0.0	$0.0	$0.0
Add Back Amortization	$1.2	$1.2	$1.2
Capital Expenditures - Additions to Fixed Assets at Cost (Addns.)	$0.0	$0.0	$0.0
WORKING CAPITAL NEEDS:			
Accts. Receivable (Incr.) Decr.	$0.0	$0.0	$0.0
Inventory (Incr.) Decr.	$0.0	$0.0	$0.0
Deposits (Incr.) Decr.	$0.0	$0.0	$0.0
Prepaid Exp. (Incr.) Decr.	$0.0	$0.0	$0.0
Accts. Payable (Decr.) Incr.	$0.0	$0.0	$0.0
Accrued Exp. (Decr.) Incr.	$0.2	$0.0	$0.0
Total Working Capital Needs	$0.2	$0.0	$0.0
Debt/Loans (Decr.) Incr.	$0.0	$0.0	$0.0
Member Investment	($5.0)	$0.0	$0.0
Member Withdrawals	($27.8)	($22.7)	($195.6)
Cash Flow	$38.2	$104.9	$421.0
Beginning Cash	$1.6	$39.8	$144.7
Ending Cash	$39.8	$144.7	$565.7

SAMPLE STATEMENT OF FORECAST ASSUMPTIONS

Income Statement (All Calculated Annually Unless Noted):

1. Sales: Units sold 10,000 x sell price $9.99 ($119.88 per year) monthly subscription each for the first year. Second and third years to increase 20 percent and 40 percent respectively. First-year monthly sales to start at 1,000 and grow to 10,000 by the last month of the first year. Basis for number of units sold: comparable apps and market research.

2. Selling, general, and administrative expenses:

   a. Wages and salaries (use a manning schedule) for first year. May have a different manning schedule for day one versus last month of the year.

      • Marketing: $65,000

      • Software/tech: $80,000

- CFO: $90,000

- Sales executive: $95,000

- Senior management x 2: $85,000

b. Payroll tax expense (FICA (Federal Insurance Contributions Act), Workers Compensation Insurance, Unemployment Insurance Tax). Usually around 15 percent of wages and salaries.
    - $62,250

c. Liability insurance. Depends on the nature of the business, but usually amounts to $2,000 to $3,000 per year for a start-up company. Get a quote if you can.
    - $2,000

d. Expenses for phone, internet, website, etc. Quote or estimate.
    - $4,800

e. Bank service fees. Get a quote or estimate.
    - $300

f. Merchant account fees. Get a quote or estimate.
    - $51,000

g. Rent expense. Get a quote.
    - $12,000

h. Utilities expense (water and electricity). Get a quote or estimate.
    - $2,400

i. Office expenses. Get a quote or estimate.
   - $2,400

j. Advertising expenses. List and price these expenses.
   - Social: $6,000
   - Google: $98,000
   - Direct to market: $20,000

k. Legal and accounting expense. Get a quote or estimate. Be careful with these expenses—they can add up quickly.
   - $60,000

l. Licenses and permits. Get a quote or estimate.
   - N/A

m. Depreciation expense. Calculate based upon any fixed assets you acquire.
   - $24,000

n. Interest expense. Calculate based upon any borrowing you do (use a loan amortization schedule).
   - $3,600

o. Other expenses. A catch-all. Estimate.
   - N/A

Balance Sheet

1. Accounts receivable if you sell on credit. Based upon the sales forecast (one and a half to two months' sales in accounts

receivable is often a reasonable estimate). Your estimate N/A months of sales.

2. Inventory if you have a product for which you will hold inventory. Based upon N/A months of cost of sales.

3. Deposits. N/A if you rent and must make a deposit; N/A if you need to pay a deposit to a supplier to obtain products.

4. Prepaid insurance. Start with $500 if you pay for your insurance a year in advance. This prepaid insurance decreases by one-twelfth of the original figure for each month of the year. If it is just a small amount, expense it all in the month in which you purchase the insurance.

5. Fixed assets. Any major purchase such as a machine, high-value electronics equipment, etc. needed to run the business. List each, list each item's useful life in months, and provide for depreciation each month. This depreciation is an expense each month on the income statement and should be accumulated as accumulated depreciation each month on the balance sheet until the item is fully depreciated.

   • Computers and office equipment: $60,000 for five years

   • Website and app: $88,000 for five years

6. Intellectual property such as patents or a major website development or an app development might be capitalized; that is, the amount spent can be entered on the balance sheet as intangible assets and amortized over the useful life of the asset (much like purchasing a large piece of equipment and depreciating the asset over the useful life of the equipment).

   • $5,800

7. Accounts payable (if you purchase on credit). Based upon terms of purchase. If you are buying items into inventory, your accounts payable will depend upon your payment terms. Often A/P is figured at thirty days' (about four and a half weeks') cost of sales.

   - N/A

8. Current portion less long-term debt. If you choose to incur debt that will be repaid more than one year in the future, there are two entries on the balance sheet: current portion—long-term debt (amount that is paid within twelve months), and long-term debt less current portion (amount that remains to be paid after deducting the current portion). Current portion less long-term debt is part of current liabilities. Long-term debt less current portion is a part of long-term liabilities. It is best to use an amortization schedule for long-term debt. See https://www.hsh.com/amortization-calculator.html.

   - Current portion—long-term debt = $15,959.94

   - Long-term debt less current portion = $284,040.06

9. Accrued payroll expense. If you pay employees twice per month, they get paid on the fifteenth of the month for work they did through the end of the prior month. So, you owe them half a month's pay at month end, and that is an accrued payroll expense.

   - $16,000

10. Accrued payroll taxes. You owe payroll taxes for your employees, and that usually runs about 15 percent of payroll. These taxes are incurred at each month end and are paid

sometime during the following month—so accrued payroll taxes are usually about 15 percent of your month's payroll.

- $4,800

11. Equity. Usually made up of the following:

- Your equity investment (you should put some cash in the business—no lender or investor will want to invest in your business unless you also put cash in the business).

  □ $50,000

- Retained earnings (your accumulated profits and/ or losses from the start of your business; add profits or subtract losses each month from the start of your business).

  □ $379,950 (over the first three years)

- Distributions (any payouts to owners for income tax obligations or general distributions; banks do not allow for distributions other than those required to cover income tax obligations for LLCs or Sub-S companies).

  □ None

- Your total assets must equal your total liabilities and equity. When forecasting, complete the liabilities and equity part of the balance sheet first and then plug in cash to make total assets equal liabilities and equity. If cash is negative, you must solve that problem—invest more cash, borrow, cut inventory, etc.

  □ They do

STATEMENT OF FORECAST ASSUMPTIONS TEMPLATE

[Date]*

Note*: If your organization form is an LLC or a Sub-S corporation, your year-end must be December 31. Also, if your business form is a Sub-S or an LLC, the company does not pay income taxes—profits are distributed to owners in proportion to their ownership percentage, and the individuals pay taxes on profits when they submit their personal tax returns. The company should make distributions from profits to cover the owners' income tax obligations created by the LLC.

Income Statement

1. Sales: Units sold _____ x sell price _____each for first year. Second and third years to increase ____ percent and ____ percent respectively. First-year monthly sales to start at _____ and grow to ____ by the last month of the first year. Basis for number of units sold: _____

    _____.

2. If your business is an app, your sales could be your fees from a customer downloading your app. In other words, app price $_____ per download x number of downloads = sales. Also, if you have advertising as an income stream, the sales would include value of the ad per download ($_____) x number of downloads = sales.

3. If you are selling a product, you will have cost of sales ___ percent of net sales. Or unit cost of sales _____ units sold for first year. Etc.

4. Selling, general, and administrative expenses:

   a. Wages and salaries (use a manning schedule) for first year. May have a different manning schedule for day one versus last month of the year.

   b. Payroll tax expense (FICA, Workers Compensation Insurance, Unemployment Insurance Tax). Usually around 15 percent of wages and salaries.

   c. Liability insurance. Depends on the nature of the business, but usually amounts to $2,000 to $3,000 per year for a start-up company. Get a quote if you can.

   d. Expenses for phone, internet, website, etc. Quote or estimate.

   e. Bank service fees. Get a quote or estimate.

   f. Merchant account fees. Get a quote or estimate.

   g. Rent expense. Get a quote.

h. Utilities expense (water and electricity). Get a quote or estimate.

i. Office expenses. Get a quote or estimate.

j. Advertising expenses. List and price these expenses.

k. Legal and accounting expense. Get a quote or estimate. Be careful with these expenses—they can add up quickly.

l. Licenses and permits. Get a quote or estimate.

m. Depreciation expense. Calculate based upon any fixed assets you acquire.

n. Interest expense. Calculate based upon any borrowing you do (use a loan amortization schedule).

o. Other expense. A catch-all. Estimate.

Balance Sheet

1. Accounts receivable if you sell on credit. Based upon sales forecast (one and a half to two months' sales in accounts receivable is often a reasonable estimate). Your estimate _____ months of sales.

2. Inventory if you have a product for which you will hold inventory. Based upon _____ months of cost of sales.

3. Deposits. _____ if you rent and have to make a deposit. _____ if you need to pay a deposit to a supplier to obtain products.

4. Prepaid insurance. Start with _____ if you pay for your insurance a year in advance. This prepaid insurance decreases

by one-twelfth of the original figure for each month of the year. If it is just a small amount, expense it all in the month in which you purchase the insurance.

5. Fixed assets. Any major purchase such as a machine, high-value electronics equipment, etc. needed to run the business. List each, list each item's useful life in months, and provide for depreciation each month. This depreciation is an expense each month on the income statement and should be accumulated as accumulated depreciation each month on the balance sheet until the item is fully depreciated.

6. Intellectual property such as patents or a major website development or an app development might be capitalized; that is, the amount spent can be entered on the balance sheet as intangible assets and amortized over the useful life of the asset (much like purchasing a large piece of equipment and depreciating the asset over the useful life of the equipment).

7. Accounts payable (if you purchase on credit). Based upon terms of purchase. If you are buying items into inventory, your accounts payable will depend upon your payment terms. Often A/P is figured at thirty days' cost of sales.

8. Current portion less long-term debt. If you choose to incur debt that will be repaid more than one year in the future, there are two entries on the balance sheet: current portion less long-term debt (amount that is paid within twelve months), and long-term debt less current portion (amount that remains to be paid after deducting the current portion). Current portion less long-term debt is part of current liabilities. Long-term debt less current portion is a part of long-term liabilities. It

is best to use an amortization schedule for long-term debt. See https://www.hsh.com/amortization-calculator.html.

9. Accrued payroll expense. If you pay employees twice per month, they get pay on the fifteenth of the month for work they did through the end of the prior month. So you owe them half a month's pay at month end, and that is an accrued payroll expense.

10. Accrued payroll taxes. You owe payroll taxes for your employees, and that usually runs about 15 percent of payroll. These taxes are incurred at each month end and are paid sometime during the following month—so accrued payroll taxes are usually about 15 percent of your month's payroll.

11. Equity. Usually made up of the following:

    a. Your equity investment (you should put some cash in the business—no lender or investor will want to invest in your business unless you also put cash in the business).

    b. Retained earnings (your accumulated profits and/or losses from the start of your business; add profits or subtract losses each month from the start of your business).

    c. Distributions (any payouts to owners for income tax obligations or general distributions; banks generally do not allow for distributions other than those required to cover income tax obligations for LLCs or Sub-S companies).

12. Your total assets must equal your total liabilities and equity. When forecasting, complete the liabilities and equity part of the balance sheet first and then plug cash to make total assets equal liabilities and equity. If cash is negative, you have to solve that problem—invest more cash, borrow, cut inventory, etc.

HOW TO WRITE A BUSINESS PLAN FOR A NEW VENTURE

James Hunter and Steven C. Michael

Six Important Tips before You Start!

1. The business plan should tell a compelling story about your venture, explaining who, what, when, where, how, and why.

2. Your plan should be focused and clear. It is not about the number of pages or style of the cover.

3. Consider the audience for the plan—their sophistication, background, and experience—and write with that audience in mind. The usual audience is an equity investor with general business and financial acumen but not necessarily technical depth or industry knowledge. Modifications may be required in length or depth for other uses and audiences.

4. The plan should define specific business objectives and goals with general parameters to guide the organization.

5. Writing a business plan should force logic and discipline into a business.

6. A good business plan is a living document; it should be updated regularly. Also, previous forecasts of progress or financials should be monitored and evaluated. "Plan the work and work the plan."

Executive Summary

This section should

- be written last;

- provide an enthusiastic snapshot of your company, explaining who you are, what you do and why;

- explain how you are financing the venture and what outside financing you seek; and

- be less than two pages in length.

After reviewing this section, the reader should

- want to learn more about your business;

- have a basic understanding of your company; and

- be informed enough to seriously consider an investment in your company.

Venture Description and Vision

This section should include the following:

- Mission statement (business purpose)

- Company vision (statement about company growth)

- Venture goals and objectives

- Anticipated timeline and key milestones

- Brief history of the venture

- Anticipated exit, harvest, or other liquidity event if equity investment is sought

- List of key venture principals

After reviewing this section, the reader should know the following:

- What the venture is and what it stands for

- Your perception of the company's growth and potential

- Specific goals and objectives of the venture

- Background information about the company

- Timeline and key milestones for the company

Description of the Market, the Need, and the Customers

This section should

- describe your venture industry and outlook;

- define the critical needs of your perceived or existing market, describe how this need is being met today, and disclose in what way the need is unmet;

- identify your target market;

- provide a general profile of your targeted customers; and

- describe what share of the market you currently have and/or anticipate.

After reviewing this section, the reader should know the following:

- Basic information about the industry you operate in and the customer needs you are fulfilling

- The key user benefit

- The scope and share of your venture's market as well as who your target customers are (provide a short-run and a long-run estimate)

PRO TIPS:

- Provide a short-run and a long-run estimate of market size. What trends or macroeconomic forces will drive growth?

- Focus on the user and the key benefit. The technology or product is much less interesting than most entrepreneurs think.

- Evidence of interest or demand from well-regarded sources is always valuable.

Description of Products and Services

This section should

- explain how your product and its features will address customers' unmet needs;

- specifically describe all of your products and services; be sure to include anything that might generate a revenue stream (e.g., selling extended warranties along with electronic products);

- give a progress report on the design and development of the product and its associated technology; if applicable, offer a short layman's summary of underlying technology;

- explain how your products and services are competitive;

- tell what your competitive edge is;

- identify intellectual property created or to be created (patents, copyrights, trademarks—Have you filed?);

- if applicable, show illustrations of your products: sketches, photos, mechanical CAD drawing, brochures, detailed product literature, other product descriptions, (links to) videos, prototypes, web pages and wireframes; and

- describe issues likely to arise in scaling the product.

After reviewing this section, the reader should know the following:

- Why you are in business.

- What your products and services are and how much they sell for.

- How and why your products and services are competitive.

- Your competitive edge.

Marketing and Sales Strategy

This section should

- identify and describe your market—who your customers are and what the demand is for your products and services;

- show a summary of your market research (What do the results show?);

- describe your channels of distribution and/or e-commerce site;

- explain your sales strategy, specific to pricing, promotion, products, and place (four Ps);

- explain how customers will be initially informed of your product and how those customers will be retained;

- explain how relevant decision makers within customer organizations will be identified, if appropriate (who can actually spend money in a hospital is a complex question);

- describe your plan for after-sale service (and follow-up sales);

- list your website and describe your social media plan for the company; and

- describe your competitors; if location is important, show on a map where you are and where competitors are located.

After reviewing this section, the reader should know the following:
- Who your market is and how you will reach it.

- How your company will apply pricing, promotion, product differentiation, and channels of distribution to sell your products and services competitively.

Operations / Manufacturing / Service Strategy

This section should
- identify and describe key components and people your product requires;

- tell which components will be purchased and which will be built in house;

- describe your source for labor, the relative skill levels required, and your training plan for employees;

- identify key suppliers and discuss their capabilities relative to the venture; and

- describe your plan for quality control and your plan to obtain relevant supplier certifications (e.g., ISO 9000).

After reviewing this section, the reader should know the following:

- That your venture can deliver on the product promise it is making at a level appropriate to the desired market.

- That your venture can attract necessary labor.

- The general flow of operations within the firm.

PRO TIP: OPERATIONS

- This section is more common with physical products rather than services or digital products. As a matter of style, for those types of ventures sometimes these details can be incorporated into the "Organization and Management" section below. However, how the venture will hire skilled labor and how training will be conducted should be included in any plan.

Organization and Management

This section should

- provide a description of how your company is organized as well as an organization chart, if available;

- describe the legal structure of your venture (remember that to shield owners from personal liability, the organization legal structure should avoid sole proprietorships and simple partnerships);

- describe in specific terms the ownership structure and how equity is currently distributed;

- identify necessary or special licenses and/or permits your venture requires (Have these been obtained?);

- provide a brief bio description of key managers within the company;

- identify key outside advisors if appropriate (e.g., consulting scientists, advisors, specialists, mentors, patent attorneys);

- describe key roles that will be filled as the company grows;

- describe all operating aspects of your venture (facility layout, hours of operation, staffing schedules, equipment required, suppliers, etc.) if not discussed in a separate section;

- discuss hiring and training plans for general employees in labor-intensive businesses if not discussed in a separate section; and

- prove that you know this business (your key managers have necessary experience and/or you have a board of advisors with the necessary experience).

After reviewing this section, the reader should know the following:

- The legal form of ownership for your venture

- Who the leaders are in your venture as well as their roles

- The general flow of operations within the firm (if not discussed in a separate section)

- How essential labor will be attracted to join the organization

- Details on equipment, suppliers, operational days and times, facilities layouts, etc.

PRO TIP: MANAGEMENT TEAM

- Be sure to demonstrate complementary skills among the management team. As one example, typically one person handles outside duties (sales, marketing, public relations) while another handles internal operations (service or product design and delivery).

- Some potential investors will not invest in a new company that does not have someone who has 51-plus percent voting control. They say that they don't want to have to deal with a "committee." Keep this in mind as initial equity is allocated.

- Any prior significant commitment of equity or borrowing should be noted here and in the financial section.

Risk Assessment

This section should

- identify and review sources of risk to the success of the plan, including but not limited to competitive, legal/regulatory, social/societal, macroeconomic, technical and technological, personnel, and cash flow;

- assess their likelihood;

- judge their impact; and

- suggest methods of avoidance, mitigation, or insurance.

After reading this section, the reader should

- be aware of risks facing the venture and be able to judge the effectiveness of the venture's plan to meet those risks should they arise.

PRO TIPS: RISK ASSESSMENT

- Risk is the product of the probability of an outcome and the severity of its impact.

- Thus, any risk that threatens the venture's survival should be discussed.

- Specificity is much more valuable than generalities. "Customers won't buy" is a risk to any business. "Customers won't buy due to the novelty of the technology" is a more specific risk that allows for plans to be made to address the risk. Also, discuss risks that are not covered elsewhere in the plan (e.g., an alternative technology proves superior).

- Risks can be positive! Present those as well.

Financial Forecast

For a new venture, this section should include the following:

- Estimate of start-up costs.

- Projected balance sheet (three years forward, by month for the first year).

- Projected income statement (three years forward, by month for the first year).

- Projected cash flow statement (three years forward, by month for the first year).

- A statement of assumptions describing how you arrived at each major item in the income statement and on the balance sheet.

- A detailed list of capital requirements, investment requested, and specific purpose for funds raised.

- Breakeven analysis, sensitivity analysis, and worst case.

After reviewing this section, the reader should

- have a good understanding regarding the financial capacity and/or projections for your company.

PRO TIPS: FINANCIAL FORECAST

- You may MARKET the truth, but you may not LIE. Make responsible forecasts that are consistent with the information available, business experience, and common sense.

- Forecasted numbers will be compared, where possible, to industry numbers and experience. A plan that forecasts winning 90 percent of an established market in the first two years is highly implausible. A plan that forecasts costs that are 50 percent of established competitors is equally implausible.

- The assumptions are the most crucial part of the plan, because they drive the forecasts. Be explicit about your assumptions, and justify them extensively.

- Investors will judge your credibility on all issues with your ability to meet or exceed these forecasts. Underpromising and overdelivering is the best strategy.

- In its early years, a successful venture often generates more demand for cash than it receives from operations. Success risks "growing broke." Plan for working capital and expansion funds.

- Work in hundreds or thousands of dollars, as appropriate for the scale of the venture. Forecasts are not accurate to the dollar and should not be reported to that precision.

Generate Business Plan

Include the following on the front page of your plan:

- Company name

- Street address

- City, state, and zipcode

- Phone number

- Email address

- Web address

- Contact information for the entrepreneurial team (always include résumés of key personnel in the appendix)

Style advice:

- Include a table of contents after the front page.

- Remember that vigorous writing is concise. Use clear prose. Omit needless words.

- Use headings, subheadings, graphics, and bulleted/numbered lists generously but thoughtfully.

- Ten to forty pages is typical, but length depends upon the venture and the audience.

□ Proofread and spellcheck **twice** before submission to any audience.

□ Include a footer with page numbers, the company name, and the date.

- "Break any of these rules [in this guide] sooner than say anything outright barbarous" (George Orwell).

PRO TIPS: OVERALL FOR THE BUSINESS PLAN

GOOD NEWS	BAD NEWS
Evidence of customer acceptance	A product (rather than customer) orientation
Evidence of focus	A "prepackaged" plan
Management team suited to the opportunity	Unrealistic financial projections
Proprietary position or technology	Failure to acknowledge critical risks
Appreciation of investors' needs	Plans to "educate" the market
Credible financials	
Management with proven sales skills	

Authors' note: This document was prepared as a resource for students, alumni, and friends of the University of Wisconsin–Milwaukee. It is intended as a general reference, applicable in a wide range of circumstances. It is intended as a guideline, not a template. No template fits all ventures but does seek to cover each relevant point above. Also, directions for course projects or campus competitions may modify these guidelines and this format.

Good luck, and happy venturing!

NEW VENTURE IDEATION AWARD–JUDGE'S EVALUATION FORM

Plan name: _____

Judge name: _____

Part 1: Written Business Plan

Please evaluate the written business plan on the following aspects: (Rating system: 1 = very poor, 2 = poor, 3 = fair, 4 = adequate, 5 = good, 6 = very good, 7 = excellent)

Please consider the following questions in your evaluation:

- Is this area covered in adequate detail?

- Does the plan show a clear understanding of the elements that should be addressed?

- Are the assumptions realistic and reasonable?

- Are the risks identified and the ability to manage those risks addressed?

1. EXECUTIVE SUMMARY

1   2   3   4   5   6   7

(Clear, exciting, and effective as a stand-alone overview of the plan.)

Comments/questions: _____

_____

_____

2. MARKET ANALYSIS AND STRATEGY

1   2   3   4   5   6   7

(Analysis of size, growth, trends, market segments, customers, and competition. Convincing description of target market, product/ service, pricing, distribution, sales, advertising, and promotion.)

Comments/questions: _____

_____

_____

3. COMPETITIVE ADVANTAGE

1   2   3   4   5   6   7

(Resources and capabilities, barriers that can be established, sustainability.)

Comments/questions: _____

_____

_____

4. OPERATIONAL PLAN / ORGANIZATION

1   2   3   4   5   6   7

(Plan for production/delivery of product or service, cost, operating complexity, required resources; backgrounds of key individuals, organization structure, board of advisors.)

Comments/questions: _____

_____

_____

5. FINANCIAL PLAN

1   2   3   4   5   6   7

(Consistent with plan and effective in capturing financial performance. Key assumptions of risks, growth, margins, major expenditures, and seasonality are clearly and realistically represented.)

Comments/questions: _____

_____

_____

6. BREVITY AND CLARITY

1   2   3   4   5   6   7

(Clearly written with a logical flow and minimal redundancy. Good use of graphics, charts, and tables.)

Comments/questions: _____

_____

_____

Part 2: Presentation

Please evaluate the business plan presentation on the following aspects: (Rating system: 1 = very poor, 2 = poor, 3 = fair, 4 = adequate, 5 = good, 6 = very good, 7 = excellent)

1   FORMAL PRESENTATION

a. Materials presented in a clear, logical form

1   2   3   4   5   6   7

b. Ability to relate need for the company with meaningful examples and practical applications

1   2   3   4   5   6   7

c. Ability to maintain judges' interest

1   2   3   4   5   6   7

d. Quality of visual aids

1   2   3   4   5   6   7

2   QUESTIONS AND ANSWERS

a. Ability to understand judges' questions

1   2   3   4   5   6   7

b. Ability to appropriately respond to judges' questions with substantive answers

1   2   3   4   5   6   7

c. Poise and confidence (ability to think effectively on their feet)

1   2   3   4   5   6   7

Comments/questions: _____

_____

_____

Strengths of presentation: _____

Weaknesses of presentation: _____

Part 3: Overall Viability of Company

Please evaluate the viability of the venture on the following aspects: (Rating system: 1 = very poor, 2 = poor, 3 = fair, 4 = adequate, 5 = good, 6 = very good, 7 = excellent)

MARKET OPPORTUNITY

1   2   3   4   5   6   7

(A clear market need is presented as well as a way to take advantage of that need.)

UNIQUE BENEFITS

1   2   3   4   5   6   7

(The company provides something novel/unique/special that differentiates it in the market.)

COMPETITIVE ADVANTAGE

1   2   3   4   5   6   7

(The major competitors are described. The competitive advantage is sustainable.)

ORGANIZATION

1   2   3   4   5   6   7

(Team can effectively develop the company or understands the additions to the organization that are required. Team can handle the risks associated with the venture.)

FINANCIAL UNDERSTANDING

1   2   3   4   5   6   7

(The financial projections are realistic. The key assumptions are explained and are reasonable.)

INVESTMENT OPPORTUNITY

1   2   3   4   5   6   7

(The business represents a real investment opportunity in which you would hypothetically consider investing.)

Venture strengths: _____

Venture weaknesses: _____

BYGRAVE AND ZACHARAKIS'S OPPORTUNITY CHECKLIST

Opportunity Checklist[26]

Project descriptive name: _____

Project leader name: _____

Place an "x" before the appropriate phrase in either the "Stronger Opportunities" or "Weaker Opportunities" column:

---

26   A. Zacharakis, A. Corbett, and W. Bygrave, *Entrepreneurship,* 5th Edition (New York: Wiley, 2020).

EVALUATION CRITERIA	STRONGER OPPORTUNITIES	WEAKER OPPORTUNITIES
CUSTOMER		
Identifiable	Primary target audience	Secondary target audience
Demographics	Clearly defined and focused	Fuzzy definition and unfocused
Psychographics	Clearly defined and focused	Fuzzy definition and unfocused
TRENDS		
Macro market	Multiple and converging	Few and disparate
Target market	Multiple and converging	Few and disparate
Window of opportunity	Opening	Closing
Market structures	Emerging/fragmented	Mature/in decline
MARKET SIZE		
How many	Primary target audience	Secondary target audience
Demand	Greater than supply	Less than supply
MARKET GROWTH		
Sales growth rate	> 20 percent	< 20 percent
PRICE / FREQUENCY / VALUE		
Price	Gross margin > 40 percent	Gross margin < 40 percent
Frequency	Often and repeated	One time
Value	Fully reflected in price	Penetration pricing
Operating expenses	Large and fixed	Low and variable
Net income margin	> 10 percent	< 10 percent
Volume	Moderate	Very high

DISTRIBUTION		
Value chain position	High margin, high power	Low margin, low power
COMPETITION		
Market structure	Emerging	Mature
Direct competitors	Few	Many
Indirect competitors	Few	Many
Substitutes	Unlikely	Likely
Stealth competitors	Unlikely	Likely
KEY SUCCESS FACTORS		
Relative position	Strong	Weak
VENDORS		
Relative power	Weak	Strong
Their gross margins	Low	High
GOVERNMENT		
Regulations	Low	High
Taxes	Low	High
GLOBAL ENVIRONMENT		
Customers	Interested and accessible	Not interested or accessible
Competition	Nonexistent or weak	Existing and strong
Vendors	Eager	Unavailable
SUMMARY		
Total opportunity	Stronger	Weaker

GET IN TOUCH

James H. Hunter
jameshhunter@jameshhunter.com
414-758-0183
13855 Juneau Boulevard
Elm Grove, Wisconsin 53122

ABOUT THE AUTHOR

Jim Hunter is the Bostrom entrepreneur in residence and has taught entrepreneurship courses at the Lubar School of Business since the late 1990s. He is the president/managing member of three companies, CFO of one company, executive vice president of one company, and director of three companies/organizations. Jim has mentored students and others as they have purchased or started a business. His objective has been to help entrepreneurs create successful businesses. Jim himself bought a failing business early in his career, and he worked—unsuccessfully—to turn the company around. He lost everything he owned except for a car and a home with a mortgage. Family members went to work as Jim started three different activities to earn income to support the family (started a distribution company to sell the products previously sold in his failed business; started a management consulting business to help small businesses; started teaching at UWM). After initiating several businesses, Jim sold two of them for significant profits. He continues teaching, acting as an advisor to individuals starting and running companies, and serving on free-market-oriented nonprofit boards.

Notes

Printed in the USA
CPSIA information can be obtained
at www.ICGtesting.com
JSHW022141160124
55462JS00006B/48